TIMED READINGS PLUS

Edward Spargo

25 Two-Part Lessons
with Questions for
Building Reading Speed and Comprehension

BOOK FOUR

JAMESTOWN PUBLISHERS

a division of NTC/CONTEMPORARY PUBLISHING Group
Lincolnwood, Illinois USA

Timed Readings Plus, Book Four, Level G

ISBN: 0-89061-906-9

Published by Jamestown Publishers,
a division of NTC/Contemporary Publishing Group, Inc.,
4255 West Touhy Avenue,
Lincolnwood, Illinois, 60712 U.S.A.
©1998 by NTC/Contemporary Publishing Group, Inc.

01 02 03 04 05 06 ML 12 11 10 9 8 7 6 5 4

CONTENTS

To the Instructor

Overview

Timed Readings Plus is designed to develop both reading speed and comprehension. A timed selection in each lesson focuses on improving reading rate. A nontimed selection—the "plus" selection—follows the timed selection. The nontimed selection concentrates on building mastery in critical areas of comprehension.

The 10 books in the series span reading levels 4–13, with one book at each level. Readability of the selections was assessed by using the Fry Readability Scale. Each book contains 25 lessons; each lesson is divided into Parts A and B.

Part A includes the timed selection followed by 10 multiple-choice questions: 5 fact questions and 5 thought questions. The timed selection is 400 words long and contains subject matter that is factual, nonfiction, and textbook-like. Because everyone—regardless of level—reads a 400-word passage, the steps for the timed selection can be concurrent for everyone.

Part B includes the nontimed selection, which is more narrative than the timed selection. The length of the selection varies depending on the subject matter, which relates to the content of the timed selection. The nontimed selection is followed by five comprehension questions that address the following major comprehension skills: recognizing words in context, distinguishing fact from opinion, keeping events in order, making correct inferences, and understanding main ideas.

Getting Started

Begin by assigning students to a level. Students should start with a book that is one level below his or her current reading level. If a student's reading level is not known, a suitable starting point would be one or two levels below the student's present grade in school.

Teaching a Lesson: Part A

Work in each lesson begins with the timed selection in Part A. If you wish to have all the students in the class read a selection at the same time, you can coordinate the timing using the following method. Give students the signal to preview. Allow 15 seconds for this. Have students begin reading the selection at the same time. After one minute has passed, write on the chalkboard the time that has elapsed. Update the time at 10-second intervals (1:00, 1:10, 1:20, etc.). Tell the students to copy down the last time shown on the chalkboard when they finish reading. They should then record this reading time in the space designated after the selection.

If students keep track of their own reading times, have them write the times at which they start and finish reading on a separate piece of paper and then figure and record their reading time as above.

Students should now answer the ten questions that follow the Part A selection. Responses are recorded by putting an X in the box next to the student's choice of answer. Correct responses to eight or more questions indicates satisfactory comprehension and recall.

Teaching a Lesson: Part B

When students have finished Part A, they can move on to read the Part B selection. Although brief, these selections deliver all the content needed to attack the range of comprehension questions that follow.

Students next answer the comprehension questions that follow the Part B selection. Directions for answering the questions are provided with each question. Correct responses require deliberation and discrimination.

Correcting and Scoring Answers

Using the Answer Key at the back of the book, students self-score their responses to the questions in Parts A and B. Incorrect answers should be circled and the correct answer should be marked. The number of correct answers for Part A and for Part B, and the total correct answers should be tallied on the final page of the lesson.

Using the Graphs

Reading times are plotted on the Reading Rate graph at the back of the book. The legend on the graph automatically converts reading times to words-per-minute rates. Comprehension totals are plotted on the Comprehension Scores graph. Plotting automatically converts the raw scores to a comprehension percentage based on four points per correct answer.

Diagnosis and Evaluation

The Comprehension Skills Profile graph at the back of the book tracks student responses to the Part B comprehension questions. For each incorrect response, students should mark an X in the corresponding box on the graph. A column of Xs rising above other columns indicates a specific comprehension weakness. Using the profile, you can assess trends in student performance and suggest remedial work if necessary.

A student who has reached a peak in reading speed (with satisfactory comprehension) is ready to advance to the next book in the series. Before moving on to the next book, students should be encouraged to maintain their speed and comprehension on a number of lessons in order to consolidate their achievement.

How to Use This Book

Getting Started

Study Part A: Reading Faster and Better. Read and learn the steps to follow and the techniques to use to help you read more quickly and more efficiently.

Study Part B: Mastering Reading Comprehension. Learn what the five categories of comprehension are all about. Knowing what kind of comprehension response is expected from you and how to achieve that response will help you better comprehend all you read.

Working a Lesson

Find the Starting Lesson. Locate the timed selection in Part A of the lesson that you are going to read. Wait for your instructor's signal to preview the selection. Your instructor will allow you 15 seconds for previewing.

Read the Part A Selection. When your instructor gives you the signal, begin reading. Read at a faster-than-normal speed. Read carefully so that you will be able to answer questions about what you have read.

Record Your Reading Time. When you finish reading, look at the blackboard and note your reading time. Write this time at the bottom of the page on the line labeled Reading Time.

Answer the Part A Questions. Answer the ten questions that follow the selection. There are five fact questions and five thought questions. Choose the best answer to each question and put an X in that box.

Read the Part B Selection. This passage is less textbook-like and more story-like than the timed selection. Read well enough so that you can answer the questions that follow.

Answer the Part B Questions. These questions are different from traditional multiple-choice questions. In answering these questions, you must make three choices for each question. Instructions for answering each category of question are given. There are 15 responses for you to record.

Correct Your Answers. Use the Answer Key at the back of the book. For the Part A questions, circle any wrong answers and put an X in the box you should have marked. For the Part B questions, circle the wrong answer and write the correct letter next to it.

Scoring Your Work

Total Your Correct Answers. Count your correct answers for Part A and for Part B. Record those numbers on the appropriate lines at the end of the lesson. Then add these two scores to determine your total correct answers. Record that number on the appropriate line.

Plotting Your Progress

Plot Your Reading Time. Refer to the Reading Rate graph on page 116. On the vertical line that represents your lesson, put an X at the point where it intersects your reading time, shown along the left-hand side. The right-hand side of the graph will reveal your words-per-minute reading speed. Your instructor will review this graph from time to time to evaluate your progress.

Plot Your Comprehension Scores. Record your comprehension scores on the graph on page 117. On the vertical line that represents your lesson, put an X at the point where it intersects your total correct answers, shown along the left-hand side. The right-hand side of the graph will reveal your comprehension percentage. Your instructor will want to review this graph, too. Your achievement, as shown on both graphs, will determine your readiness to move on to higher and more challenging levels.

Plot Your Comprehension Skills. You will find the Comprehension Skills Profile on page 118. It is used to record your wrong answers only for the Part B questions. The five categories of questions are listed along the bottom. There are five columns of boxes, one column for each question. For every wrong answer put an X in a box for that question. Your instructor will use this graph to detect any comprehension problems you may be experiencing.

Part A: Reading Faster and Better

Step 1: Preview

When you read, do you start in with the first word, or do you look over the whole selection for a moment? Good readers preview the selection first. This helps to make them good—and fast—readers. Here are the steps to follow when previewing the timed selection in Part A of each unit.

1. Read the Title. Titles are designed not only to announce the subject, but also to make the reader think. What can you learn from the title? What thoughts does it bring to mind? What do you already know about this subject?

2. Read the First Sentence. Read the first two sentences if they are short. The opening sentence is the writer's opportunity to greet the reader. Some writers announce what they hope to tell you in the selection. Some writers tell you why they are writing. Other writers just try to get your attention.

3. Read the Last Sentence. Read the final two sentences if they are short. The closing sentence is the writer's last chance to talk to you. Some writers repeat the main idea once more. Some writers draw a conclusion—this is what they have been leading up to. Other writers summarize their thoughts; they tie all the facts together.

4. Scan the Selection. Glance through the selection quickly to see what else you can pick up. Look for anything that can help you read the selection. Are there names, dates, or numbers? If so, you may have to read more slowly. Is the selection informative—containing a lot of facts, or is it conversational—an informal discussion with the reader?

Step 2: Read for Meaning

When you read, do you just see words? Are you so occupied reading words that you sometimes fail to get the meaning? Good readers see beyond the words—they seek the meaning. This makes them faster readers.

1. Build Concentration. You cannot read with understanding if you are not concentrating. When you discover that your thoughts are straying, correct the situation right away. Avoid distractions and distracting situations. Keep the preview information in mind. This will help to focus your attention on the selection.

2. Read in Thought Groups. A reader should strive to see words in meaningful combinations. If you see only a word at a time (called word-by-word reading), your comprehension suffers along with your speed.

3. Question the Writer. To sustain the pace you have set for yourself, and to maintain a high level of concentration and comprehension, question the writer as you read. Ask yourself such questions as, "What does this mean? How can I use this information?"

Step 3: Grasp Paragraph Sense

The paragraph is the basic unit of meaning. If you can discover quickly and understand the main point of each paragraph, you can comprehend the writer's message. Good readers know how to find the main ideas quickly. This helps to make them faster readers.

1. Find the Topic Sentence. The topic sentence, which contains the main idea, is often the first sentence of a paragraph. It is followed by sentences that support, develop, or explain the main idea. Sometimes a topic sentence comes at the end of a paragraph. When it does, the supporting details come first, building the base for the topic sentence. Some paragraphs do not have a topic sentence; all of the sentences combine to create a meaningful idea.

2. Understand Paragraph Structure. Every well-written paragraph has a purpose. The purpose may be to inform, define, explain, illustrate, and so on. The purpose should always relate the main idea and expand on it. As you read each paragraph, see how the body of the paragraph is used to tell you more about the main idea.

Step 4: Organize Facts

When you read, do you tend to see a lot of facts without any apparent connection or relationship? Understanding how the facts all fit together to deliver the writer's message is, after all, the reason for reading. Good readers organize facts as they read. This helps them to read rapidly and well.

1. Discover the Writer's Plan. Every writer has a plan or outline to follow. If you can discover the writer's method of organization, you have a key to understanding the message. Sometimes the writer gives you obvious signals. The statement, "There are three reasons . . ." should prompt you to look for a listing of the three items. Other less obvious signal words such as *moreover*, *otherwise*, and *consequently* tell you the direction the writer is taking in delivering a message.

2. Relate as You Read. As you read the selection, keep the information learned during the preview in mind. See how the writer is attempting to piece together a meaningful message. As you discover the relationship among the ideas, the message comes through quickly and clearly.

PART B: MASTERING READING COMPREHENSION

Recognizing Words in Context

Always check to see if the words around a new word—its context—can give you some clue to its meaning. A word generally appears in a context related to its meaning. If the words *soil* and *seeds* appear in an article about gardens, for example, you can assume they are related to the topic of gardens.

Suppose you are unsure of the meaning of the word *expired* in the following paragraph:

> Vera wanted to take a book out, but her library card had expired.
> She had to borrow mine because she didn't have time to renew hers.

You could begin to figure out the meaning of *expired* by asking yourself, "What could have happened to Vera's library card that would make her have to borrow someone else's card?" You might realize that if she had to renew her card, it must have come to an end or run out. This would lead you to conclude that the word *expired* must mean to come to an end or run out. You would be right. The context suggested the meaning to you.

Context can also affect the meaning of a word you know. The word key, for instance, has many meanings. There are musical keys, door keys, and keys to solving a mystery. The context in which key occurs will tell you which meaning is right.

Sometimes a hard word will be explained by the words that immediately follow it. The word *grave* in the following sentence might give you trouble:

> He looked grave; there wasn't a trace of a smile on his lips.

You can figure out that the second part of the sentence explains the word *grave*: "wasn't a trace of a smile" indicates a serious look, so grave must mean serious.

The subject of a sentence and your knowledge about that subject might also help you determine the meaning of an unknown word. Try to decide the meaning of the word *revive* in the following sentence:

> Sunshine and water will revive those drooping plants.

The sentence is about giving plants light and water. You may know that plants need light and water to be healthy. If you know that drooping plants are not healthy, you can figure out that revive means to bring back to health.

Distinguishing Fact from Opinion

Every day you are called upon to sort out fact and opinion. When a friend says she saw Mel Gibson's greatest movie last night, she is giving you her opinion. When she says she saw Mel Gibson's latest movie, she may be stating a fact. The fact can be proven—you can check to confirm or verify that the movie is indeed Mel Gibson's most recent film. The opinion can be disputed—ask around and others may not agree about the film's unqualified greatness. Because much of what you read and hear contains both facts and opinions, you need to be able to tell them apart. You need the skill of distinguishing fact from opinion.

Facts are statements that can be proven true. The proof must be objective and verifiable. You must be able to check for yourself to confirm a fact.

Look at the following facts. Notice that they can be checked for accuracy and confirmed. Suggested sources for verification appear in parentheses.

- In 1998 Bill Clinton was President of the United States. (Consult news papers, news broadcasts, election results, etc.)

- Earth revolves around the Sun. (Look it up in encyclopedias or astrological journals; ask knowledgeable people.)

- Dogs walk on four legs. (See for yourself.)

Opinions are statements that cannot be proven true. There is no objective evidence you can consult to check the truthfulness of an opinion. Unlike facts, opinions express personal beliefs or judgments. Opinions reveal how someone feels about a subject, not the facts about that subject. You might agree or disagree with someone's opinion, but you cannot prove it right or wrong.

Look at the following opinions. Reasons for classification as opinions appear in parentheses.

- Bill Clinton was born to be a president. (You cannot prove this by referring to birth records. There is no evidence to support this belief.)

- Intelligent life exists on other planets in our solar system. (There is no proof of this. It may be proven true some day, but for now it is just an educated guess—not a fact.)

- Dog is man's best friend. (This is not a fact; your best friend might not be a dog.)

As you read, be aware that facts and opinions are frequently mixed together. The following passage contains both facts and opinions:

> The new 2000 Cruising Yacht offers lots of real-life interior room. It features a luxuriant aft cabin, not some dim "cave." The galley comes

equipped with a full-size refrigerator and freezer. And this spacious galley has room to spare. The heads (there are two) have separate showers. The fit and finish are beyond equal and the performance is responsive and outstanding.

Did you detect that the third and fifth sentences state facts and that the rest of the sentences express opinions? Both facts and opinions are useful to you as a reader. But to evaluate what you read and to read intelligently, you need to know the difference between them.

Keeping Events in Order

Writers organize details in a pattern. They present information in a certain order. Recognizing how writers organize—and understanding that organization—can help you improve your comprehension.

When details are arranged in the precise order in which they occurred, a writer is using a chronological (or time) pattern. A writer may, however, change this order. The story may "flash back" to past events that affected the present. The story may "flash forward" to show the results of present events. The writer may move back and forth between past, present, and future to help you see the importance of events.

Making Correct Inferences

Much of what you read suggests more than it says. Writers do not always state outright what they want you to know. Frequently, they omit information that underlies the statements they make. They may assume that you already know it. They may want you to make the effort to figure out the implied information. To get the most out of what you read, you must come to an understanding about unstated information. You can do this through inference. From what is stated, you make inferences about what is not.

You make many inferences every day. Imagine, for example, that you are visiting a friend's house for the first time. You see a bag of dog food. You infer (make an inference) that the family has a dog. On another day you overhear a conversation. You catch the names of two actors and the words *scene, dialogue,* and *directing.* You infer that the people are discussing a movie or play.

In these situations and others like them, you infer unstated information from what you observe or read. Readers who cannot make inferences cannot see beyond the obvious. For the careful reader, facts are just the beginning. Facts stimulate your mind to think beyond them—to make an inference about what is meant but not stated.

The following passage is about Charles Dickens. As you read it, see how many inferences you can make.

Charles Dickens visited the United States in 1867. Wherever he went, the reception was the same. The night before, crowds arrived and lined up before the door. By morning the streets were camp-grounds, with men, women, and children sitting or sleeping on blankets. Hustlers got ten times the price of a ticket. Once inside, audiences were surprised to hear their favorite Dickens characters speak with an English accent. After 76 readings Dickens boarded a ship for England. When his fellow passengers asked him to read, he said he'd rather be put in irons!

Did you notice that many inferences may be drawn from the passage? Dickens attracted huge crowds. From that fact you can infer that he was popular. His English accent surprised audiences. You can infer that many didn't know he was English. Hustlers got high prices for tickets. This suggests that "scalping" tickets is not new. Dickens refused to read on the ship. You can infer that he was exhausted and tired of reading aloud to audiences. Those are some obvious inferences that can be made from the passage. More subtle ones can also be made; however, if you see the obvious ones, you understand how inferences are made.

Be careful about the inferences you make. One set of facts may suggest several inferences. Not all of them will be correct; some will be faulty inferences. The correct inference is supported by enough evidence to make it more likely than other inferences.

Understanding Main Ideas

The main idea tells who or what is the subject of the paragraph or passage. The main idea is the most important idea, the idea that provides purpose and direction. The rest of the paragraph or passage explains, develops, or supports the main idea. Without a main idea, there would only be a collection of unconnected thoughts. It would be like a handle and a bowl without the "idea cup," or bread and meat without the "idea sandwich."

In the following passage, the main idea is printed in italics. As you read, observe how the other sentences develop or explain the main idea.

Typhoon Chris hit with full fury today on the central coast of Japan. Heavy rain from the storm flooded the area. High waves carried many homes into the sea. People now fear that the heavy rains will cause mudslides in the central part of the country. The number of people killed by the storm may climb past the 200 mark by Saturday.

In this paragraph, the main idea statement appears first. It is followed by sentences that explain, support, or give details. Sometimes the main idea appears at the end of a paragraph. Writers often construct that type of paragraph when their purpose is to persuade or convince. Readers may be more open to a new idea if the reasons for it are presented first. As you read the following paragraph, think about the overall impact of the supporting ideas. Their purpose is to convince the reader that the main idea in the last sentence should be accepted.

> Last week there was a head-on collision at Huntington and Canton streets. Just a month ago a pedestrian was struck there. Fortunately, she was only slightly injured. In the past year there have been more accidents there than at any other corner in the city. In fact, nearly 10 percent of all city accidents occur there. This intersection is dangerous, and a traffic signal should be installed there before a life is lost.

The details in the paragraph progress from least important to most important. They achieve their full effect in the main idea statement at the end.

In many cases, the main idea is not expressed in a single sentence. In these cases, the reader is called upon to interpret all of the ideas expressed and decide upon a main idea. Read the following paragraph:

> The American author Jack London was once a pupil at the Cole Grammar School in Oakland, California. Each morning the class sang a song. When the teacher noticed that Jack wouldn't sing, she sent him to the principal. He returned to class with a note. It said that he could be excused from singing if he would write an essay every morning.

In this paragraph the reader has to interpret the individual ideas and decide on a main idea. This main idea seems reasonable: Jack London's career as a writer began with a "punishment" in grammar school.

Understanding the concept of the main idea and knowing how to find it is important. Transferring that understanding to your reading and study is also important.

In the distant past before any sciences existed, the beginnings of the world and of society were explained by stories called myths. A culture's collective myths are known as its mythology. Myths try to answer basic human questions about existence. Where did the world come from? How did people originate? Why is there evil in the world? What characteristics make up the perfect human? What happens to people after they die? Such questions have persisted throughout human history in every culture. Myths also try to account for a society's customs and rituals.

Traditionally, myths did not originate in written form. They developed slowly as an oral tradition that was handed down over generations. Early people looked around and tried to make sense of the world around them. They tried to imagine how it could have come into being. They wondered what kind of godlike or supernatural beings could be responsible for creating and controlling the world.

The elders of society who were considered wise pondered what they saw. They came up with their own conclusions about natural events and human behavior. They developed stories that explained how such things came to be. They had to account for everything that happened—from the origin of the world up to and including the present. These accounts, passed down in story form, were eventually accepted as traditional truth. Much later the stories were written down.

Although mythmaking is an ancient practice, it is not a practice limited to people who lived thousands of years ago. People continue to create myths to explain their world. The American West of the 19th century has been a favorite subject on which to build modern myths. The Wild West was a reality, complete with cowboys, Indians, outlaws, and federal marshals. The stories presented in Western fiction and in the movies and on television, however, are highly romanticized versions of a reality that was far less glamorous. These stories help Americans understand their culture.

Mythmaking has traditionally looked to the past to try to make sense out of the present. Some modern myths look instead to the future. Storytellers make use of the countless inventions of the last few centuries to give vivid depictions of what Earth may be like hundreds of years from now. They imagine life on worlds billions of light-years away in space or far in the future. These stories also help cultures understand their world.

Reading Time _____

Recalling Facts

1. Traditionally, myths were
   - ❏ a. written down.
   - ❏ b. passed on orally.
   - ❏ c. part of religious ceremonies.

2. A culture's collective myths are known as its
   - ❏ a. history.
   - ❏ b. mythology.
   - ❏ c. scientific truth.

3. Myths are best described as
   - ❏ a. realistic stories about important events.
   - ❏ b. fanciful tales of the distant past and future.
   - ❏ c. stories that try to answer basic questions about the world.

4. Traditionally, myths
   - ❏ a. look to the present to make sense out of the past.
   - ❏ b. look to the past to make sense out of the present.
   - ❏ c. describe future events.

5. A favorite subject on which to build modern myths is
   - ❏ a. traffic jams.
   - ❏ b. the American West of the 19th century.
   - ❏ c. the invention of rubber.

Understanding Ideas

6. Mythmaking has persisted throughout history, which suggests that
   - ❏ a. people's basic needs have not changed very much.
   - ❏ b. ancient people had nothing in common with people today.
   - ❏ c. myths have no scientific basis.

7. The popularity of myths is the result of
   - ❏ a. a movement away from scientific thought.
   - ❏ b. a need for people to explain what they see around them.
   - ❏ c. people taking things for granted.

8. From the article you can conclude that the first myths were passed on orally because
   - ❏ a. they changed constantly.
   - ❏ b. people had no knowledge of writing.
   - ❏ c. they were acted out.

9. A myth would most likely describe the moon as a
   - ❏ a. satellite circling the Earth.
   - ❏ b. goddess living in the sky.
   - ❏ c. lifeless wasteland covered with dust.

10. From the article you can conclude that mythmaking may be thought of as a
    - ❏ a. pastime of ancient people.
    - ❏ b. practice limited to advanced cultures.
    - ❏ c. common activity among all people.

Raven and the Haida People

People have always told stories that explain how the world came to be and how people arrived on it. On the Northwest Coast of North America, Native Americans tell about Raven. Raven is a giant bird who can change himself into human form by pushing up his beak and shrugging off his wings, which then become a cloak. The stories also assure the people that Raven takes special care of those who venerate him.

According to tradition, the universe always existed as a wide ocean that covered swampy ground. Birds and sea creatures lived in and around it. Raven made the earth by scooping up pebbles with his beak and dropping them into the ocean. When the earth was big enough, Raven swooped down and walked on the shore, looking out at the vast ocean and feeling lonely.

Then he began to hear tiny voices. They seemed to be coming from a clam shell at his feet. Raven pried open the clam shell with his mighty claws and peered in. Inside the clam shell were people. As the story goes, Raven coaxed them out of the shell and set them on the land, and they were the first people of the Haida tribe of the Northwest Coast.

1. **Recognizing Words in Context**

Find the word *venerate* in the passage. One definition below is a *synonym* for that word; it means the same or almost the same thing. One definition is an *antonym*; it has the opposite or nearly opposite meaning. The other has a completely different meaning. Label the definitions S for *synonym*, A for *antonym*, and D for *different*.

_____ a. ignores
_____ b. honors
_____ c. sees

2. **Distinguishing Fact from Opinion**

Two of the statements below present *facts*, which can be proved correct. The other statement is an *opinion*, which expresses someone's thoughts or beliefs. Label the statements F for *fact* and O for *opinion*.

_____ a. People tell tales to explain how the world came to be.
_____ b. Northwest Coast people tell about Raven.
_____ c. Raven is a giant bird who can change into human form.

3. Keeping Events in Order

Label the statements below 1, 2, and 3 to show the order in which the events happened.

_____ a. Raven dropped pebbles into the sea.

_____ b. Raven walked on the shore.

_____ c. Raven helped people out of the clam shell.

4. Making Correct Inferences

Two of the statements below are correct *inferences*, or reasonable guesses. They are based on information in the passage. The other statement is an incorrect, or faulty, inference. Label the statements C for *correct* inference and F for *faulty* inference.

_____ a. The Raven myth explains the existence of the Haida people.

_____ b. Raven is a supernatural being.

_____ c. Raven is not important to the Haida today.

5. Understanding Main Ideas

One of the statements below expresses the main idea of the passage. One statement is too general, or too broad. The other explains only part of the passage; it is too narrow. Label the statements M for *main idea*, B for *too broad*, and N for *too narrow*.

_____ a. Myths explain different things.

_____ b. Raven started the Haida tribe by coaxing the first people out of a clam shell.

_____ c. The Haida people explain their emergence into the world through a myth involving Raven.

Correct Answers, Part A _____

Correct Answers, Part B _____

Total Correct Answers _____

More than 10,000 species of crickets, grasshoppers, and katydids live throughout the world. These insects normally have two pairs of wings. The outer, forward wings are thick and tough and are held stiff and motionless. They protect the filmy rear wings, which move when the insect is flying. When the rear wings are not in use, they fold up like fans and lie along the back beneath the forward pair. Some species are wingless or have small wings that are useless for flying.

Most species have legs that are highly efficient for jumping. The front and middle pairs are short. The rear legs are longer than the entire body and are very powerful. The upper section of the hind legs has especially strong muscles. The lower part has sharp spines located at the end near the foot. When a grasshopper, for example, prepares to jump, it digs the spines into the ground. Then it straightens its legs and shoots forward like a released spring. Some kinds of grasshoppers can jump more than 100 times their length.

Crickets, grasshoppers, and katydids are among the noisiest and most musical of the insects. The chirp of crickets has been considered a blessing in Europe and America. The Chinese, who believe the cricket to be a creature of good omen, predict good luck for a house that has many crickets.

These insects produce sound by rubbing certain parts of the body against other parts. In most species, only the males make sound, as a means of attracting mates or as identification to other males. The cricket's distinctive song is produced when males scrape the rough surfaces of their wing covers together. Grasshoppers and katydids—members of the grasshopper family—also use their wings to make the chirruping noise. Like crickets, katydids rub their wings against one another. Grasshoppers, however, usually rub a leg in a sawing motion across a wing to create the sound. Katydids are so named because their song is said to sound like "Katy did, Katy did."

These insects are well equipped for hearing and seeing. They have large, compound eyes, which are groups of seeing units. These allow them to see in all directions at once. Two structures that act as ears are located on the legs or on the body. The antennae, or "feelers," are located on the head; they are organs of smell, touch, and sometimes hearing.

Reading Time _____

Recalling Facts

1. The number of species of crickets, grasshoppers, and katydids is over
   - ❏ a. 5,000.
   - ❏ b. 8,000.
   - ❏ c. 10,000.

2. These insects normally have
   - ❏ a. one pair of wings.
   - ❏ b. two pairs of wings.
   - ❏ c. three pairs of wings.

3. To the Chinese, crickets are a symbol of
   - ❏ a. bad luck.
   - ❏ b. good luck.
   - ❏ c. music.

4. The eyes of crickets, grasshoppers, and katydids are
   - ❏ a. large and compound.
   - ❏ b. small.
   - ❏ c. usually closed.

5. The longest set of legs of these insects are found
   - ❏ a. at the front of the body.
   - ❏ b. in the middle of the body.
   - ❏ c. at the rear of the body.

Understanding Ideas

6. From the article you can conclude that crickets, grasshoppers, and katydids have no
   - ❏ a. vocal chords.
   - ❏ b. heads.
   - ❏ c. feet.

7. It is likely that compound eyes help insects
   - ❏ a. locate their prey.
   - ❏ b. predict the weather.
   - ❏ c. build nests.

8. From the article you can conclude that insects have
   - ❏ a. two legs.
   - ❏ b. four legs.
   - ❏ c. six legs.

9. From the article you can conclude that an insect's body parts are
   - ❏ a. much like those of humans.
   - ❏ b. very different from those of humans.
   - ❏ c. identical to each other's.

10. The sounds produced by certain insects serves primarily as
    - ❏ a. entertainment.
    - ❏ b. a warning signal.
    - ❏ c. identification.

2   B   Summer of the Locusts

There was a haze in the Kansas air that hot August day in 1874. As Mary Nelson looked across the fields, the sun began to grow dim. "I think a dust storm's coming, Mother!" Mary shouted. As her mother stepped outside, the dark cloud drew nearer. A pattering sound began as dark bodies dropped from the cloud and struck the ground. Within minutes, Mary and her mother were caught in a hail of falling locusts—migrating grasshoppers.

On the ground, the swarm of locusts formed a living carpet, inches deep and stretching as far as the eye could see. As the swarm moved, it began to eat. Mary held her hands over her ears to shut out the sound of millions of insect jaws at work.

"The crops!" her mother cried. "They'll eat everything! Grab blankets. We can't save the corn, but if we cover the garden, we might be able to save some vegetables."

Over the next two days, the locusts ate. They ate the corn, the garden plants, grass, weeds, and the leaves and bark of trees. When all the plantlife was gone, they attacked wooden tool handles, fence rails, and even leather harnesses. When they had eaten everything that could be eaten, they flew off.

Mary and her mother looked at the bare soil where their crops had grown. "We'll replant," her mother said. "We'll go on."

1. **Recognizing Words in Context**

   Find the word *drew* in the passage. One definition below is a *synonym* for that word; it means the same or almost the same thing. One definition is an *antonym*; it has the opposite or nearly opposite meaning. The other has a completely different meaning. Label the definitions S for *synonym*, A for *antonym*, and D for *different*.

   _____ a. moved
   _____ b. sketched
   _____ c. stopped

2. **Distinguishing Fact from Opinion**

   Two of the statements below present *facts*, which can be proved correct. The other statement is an *opinion*, which expresses someone's thoughts or beliefs. Label the statements F for *fact* and O for *opinion*.

   _____ a. The locusts ate all the plantlife.
   _____ b. Mary and her mother should move somewhere else.
   _____ c. The locusts formed a living carpet on the ground.

3. **Keeping Events in Order**

   Two of the statements below describe events that happened at the same time. The other statement describes an event that happened before or after those events. Label them S for *same time,* B for *before,* and A for *after.*

   _____ a. Dark bodies dropped from the cloud.

   _____ b. The locusts began to eat.

   _____ c. A pattering sound began.

4. **Making Correct Inferences**

   Two of the statements below are correct *inferences,* or reasonable guesses. They are based on information in the passage. The other statement is an incorrect, or faulty, inference. Label the statements C for *correct* inference and F for *faulty* inference.

   _____ a. Locusts have large appetites and eat just about anything.

   _____ b. Locusts travel in huge swarms.

   _____ c. Locusts are carried through the air by dust storms.

5. **Understanding Main Ideas**

   One of the statements below expresses the main idea of the passage. One statement is too general, or too broad. The other explains only part of the passage; it is too narrow. Label the statements M for *main idea,* B for *too broad,* and N for *too narrow.*

   _____ a. In 1874 a swarm of locusts landed on the Nelson farm and ate nearly everything.

   _____ b. After locusts eat all the plantlife, they will eat wooden tool handles, fence rails, and leather items.

   _____ c. Locust swarms have plagued human settlements since prehistoric times.

Correct Answers, Part A _____

Correct Answers, Part B _____

Total Correct Answers _____

America's Roads

The first paved road in the world is believed to have been built in about 2500 B.C. in Egypt to aid the construction of the Great Pyramids. The first organized road building was done in western Asia. The most famous road builders, however, were the Romans. They built roads for military and trade use throughout Europe and Britain.

The first major road system in the United States began to take shape in the late 18th century. Following the American Revolution, stagecoaches were in general use and there was a demand for surfaced, all-weather roads. In 1806, Congress authorized construction of the Cumberland Road. It ran between Cumberland, Maryland, and Vandalia, Illinois. The Cumberland Road opened up the American West.

At this time, many of the roads in the eastern United States were turnpikes, or toll roads. Travelers paid a fee to use them. Turnpikes were surfaced with tree trunks that were laid across the width of the road, forming a so-called corduroy road. Other roads were plank roads, paved with split logs. America's early highway designs were largely the work of Europeans. Two Scottish engineers pioneered the use of pavements built of broken stone carefully placed in layers and well compacted. In England, John Metcalf was the first engineer to design roads that had adequate drainage.

Beginning in 1910, modern road-building techniques began to evolve rapidly. Hundreds of miles of concrete and asphalt pavements were laid. In 1921, Congress made the first move toward creating a national integrated road system by passing the first federal-aid highway law. Under this law, states were eligible for financial help in building main rural roads. In turn, they were required to maintain the roads.

Today, taxes are paid by motorists when they buy gasoline, oil, tires, and other supplies. The federal government collects the taxes and places them in the Highway Trust Fund. These taxes are then distributed to the states for use in road construction and improvement. Each state also collects road-user taxes. Additional funds are raised through tolls and financial bonds.

New types of roads have been proposed for the future. Over time, heavy trucks can cause serious damage to pavements. It has been proposed that special roads be built for use only by trucks. Also proposed has been the building of an electronic highway with a remote-control system. It would automatically guide vehicles from their point of entry to the desired exit.

Reading Time _____

Recalling Facts

1. The first paved road was built in
   - ❏ a. Rome.
   - ❏ b. Greece.
   - ❏ c. Egypt.

2. Early turnpikes were surfaced with
   - ❏ a. tar.
   - ❏ b. tree trunks.
   - ❏ c. slate.

3. Money for road construction comes from
   - ❏ a. taxes and tolls paid by motorists.
   - ❏ b. property taxes.
   - ❏ c. businesses.

4. The first federal-aid highway law provided
   - ❏ a. financial help to states for building roads.
   - ❏ b. benefits for people robbed on the highways.
   - ❏ c. aid to the poor.

5. Roads built today are composed of
   - ❏ a. railroad ties.
   - ❏ b. concrete and asphalt.
   - ❏ c. bricks.

Understanding Ideas

6. From the article you can conclude that taxes paid by motorists
   - ❏ a. provide enough money to maintain our roads.
   - ❏ b. should be used for purposes other than road maintenance.
   - ❏ c. do not provide sufficient funds for road maintenance.

7. From the article you can conclude that before engineer John Metcalf designed the first roads with adequate drainage,
   - ❏ a. flooding on roads was a problem.
   - ❏ b. cars used bridges.
   - ❏ c. there were many road accidents.

8. The article wants you to understand that the U.S. highway system is
   - ❏ a. run by the states.
   - ❏ b. regulated by the government.
   - ❏ c. in danger of bankruptcy.

9. New types of roads have been proposed for the future, which suggests that
   - ❏ a. there is a need for change in road construction.
   - ❏ b. most of our roads are outdated.
   - ❏ c. our highway system is poorly managed.

10. One possible advantage of an electronic highway is that
    - ❏ a. guided vehicles would have fewer accidents.
    - ❏ b. cars would go faster.
    - ❏ c. tolls would be lower.

The Lincoln Highway

In 1912 two pioneers in the automobile business, Carl Fisher and Henry Joy, proposed building a cross-country road. Fisher and Joy planned to get the job done by 1915. People with cars would then find it easier to drive to the San Francisco Exposition. Fisher and Joy suggested calling the road the Lincoln Highway. To promote their idea, they formed the Lincoln Highway Association.

The Lincoln Highway was a rudimentary patchwork of existing roads. It wound through acres of cornfields and along the main streets of small towns. But people liked the idea. Businesses competed for an address on the Lincoln Highway.

By 1924 Iowans were paving their section of the Lincoln Highway. Farmers were moving more produce on the road, and more people were traveling by car. The idea grew, and more highways were developed.

In 1925 the United States government decided that named highways were too confusing. They began labeling them with numbers. The Lincoln Highway Association was disbanded in 1928, but work on the highway went on and people kept using the Lincoln name. Today, Interstate 80 follows much the same route as the old Lincoln Highway, the forerunner of our national highway system.

1. **Recognizing Words in Context**

   Find the word *rudimentary* in the passage. One definition below is a *synonym* for that word; it means the same or almost the same thing. One definition is an *antonym*; it has the opposite or nearly opposite meaning. The other has a completely different meaning. Label the definitions S for *synonym*, A for *antonym*, and D for *different*.

   _____ a. sophisticated
   _____ b. undeveloped
   _____ c. unplanned

2. **Distinguishing Fact from Opinion**

   Two of the statements below present *facts*, which can be proved correct. The other statement is an *opinion*, which expresses someone's thoughts or beliefs. Label the statements F for *fact* and O for *opinion*.

   _____ a. The Lincoln Highway Association was disbanded in 1928.
   _____ b. The government decided to label highways with numbers.
   _____ c. People liked the idea of the Lincoln Highway.

3. Keeping Events in Order

Label the statements below 1, 2, and 3 to show the order in which the events happened.

_____ a. The Lincoln Highway Association was formed.

_____ b. More people began to travel by car.

_____ c. Henry Joy and Carl Fisher proposed building a cross-country highway.

4. Making Correct Inferences

Two of the statements below are correct *inferences,* or reasonable guesses. They are based on information in the passage. The other statement is an incorrect, or faulty, inference. Label the statements C for *correct* inference and F for *faulty* inference.

_____ a. The Lincoln Highway was a good idea.

_____ b. The Lincoln Highway was a failure.

_____ c. Carl Fisher and Henry Joy accurately forecast an increase in cross-country travel by car.

5. Understanding Main Ideas

One of the statements below expresses the main idea of the passage. One statement is too general, or too broad. The other explains only part of the passage; it is too narrow. Label the statements M for *main idea,* B for *too broad,* and N for *too narrow.*

_____ a. The Lincoln Highway stretched across the country.

_____ b. The Lincoln Highway strung together existing roads.

_____ c. The Lincoln Highway paved the way to America's national highway system

Correct Answers, Part A _____

Correct Answers, Part B _____

Total Correct Answers _____

Deer

Members of the deer family are found throughout the Western Hemisphere, Europe, and Asia. Included among the approximately three dozen species in the deer family are wapiti, moose, and caribou. Solid horns, called antlers, distinguish most species in the deer family from the other hoofed mammals. Except for female caribou, only male deer grow antlers, which they shed each year. In contrast, both sexes of many other hoofed mammals have permanent, hollow horns. Among deer, the antlers serve as weapons. During the mating season the males fight to win the chance to breed with females. In contrast to many European and Asian species, the North American deer do not utter sounds.

Members of the deer family live in a wide variety of places, including forests, swamps, deserts, and tundra. They feed exclusively on such plant materials as grass, young shoots, twigs, and bark. Some deer travel in herds and migrate seasonally. Deer are extremely cautious animals with keen senses of smell and hearing. Most deer reach maturity in one to three years, and the female gives birth to one or two young, or, occasionally, to triplets. The young deer, called fawns, nurse for several months.

The most common deer in the eastern United States is the white-tailed deer. They range throughout eastern North America from southern Canada through Central America. In colonial times they were one of the most important wild game animals. Their meat, called venison, was a major source of food for the early settlers. Deer hides were used to make buckskin jackets, moccasins, and other leather articles. Even today the white-tailed deer is the most popular large game animal in the eastern United States.

White-tailed deer are larger in the northern part of their range where bucks, or males, often weigh more than 470 pounds (211.5 kilograms). As in most deer species, the does, or females, are somewhat smaller. Both sexes are reddish brown in summer and gray in winter. When they run, they lift their tails straight up like white flags. The young, called fawns, have reddish coats with white spots.

A buck develops a pair of spiked antlers by the fall of its second year. Between January and April the buck sheds his antlers and grows a larger set. The autumn mating season transforms timid bucks into fierce fighters. The winner in a contest of clashing antlers inherits mating privileges with the does in the vicinity.

Reading Time _____

Recalling Facts

1. Antlers are found only on
   - ❏ a. female caribou.
   - ❏ b. male deer.
   - ❏ c. male deer and female caribou.

2. The most common deer in the eastern United States are
   - ❏ a. reindeer.
   - ❏ b. white-tailed deer.
   - ❏ c. wapiti.

3. Young deer are called
   - ❏ a. does.
   - ❏ b. fawns.
   - ❏ c. bucks.

4. North American deer
   - ❏ a. are the fiercest species.
   - ❏ b. do not utter sounds.
   - ❏ c. travel constantly.

5. During mating season male deer fight
   - ❏ a. all does in the vicinity.
   - ❏ b. with each other.
   - ❏ c. fawns in the herd.

Understanding Ideas

6. We can conclude that a deer's antlers are used mainly
   - ❏ a. during mating season.
   - ❏ b. for fighting.
   - ❏ c. to make leather goods.

7. For food and clothing, early colonists depended largely on
   - ❏ a. white-tailed deer.
   - ❏ b. venison.
   - ❏ c. caribou.

8. The article wants you to understand that today deer
   - ❏ a. are a major food source.
   - ❏ b. provide much-needed hides for clothing.
   - ❏ c. are primarily considered sport for hunting.

9. Deer live in a wide variety of places, suggesting that they are
   - ❏ a. cautious.
   - ❏ b. adaptable.
   - ❏ c. limited.

10. From the article you can conclude that without antlers, young male deer would be
   - ❏ a. poor fighters.
   - ❏ b. fierce fighters.
   - ❏ c. unable to fight.

4 B Père David's Deer

In 1865 a French missionary to China named Père David saw large, handsome deer in the Royal Hunting Preserve of Beijing. His discovery proved to be a kind of deer hitherto unknown in Europe. The deer, already quite rare, had an ancient history in China. Legend said that they were harnessed to the chariots of Chinese gods.

European zoos immediately wanted the deer, and China gave some away. Then in 1900 soldiers shot the remaining deer during a rebellion. There were no more Père David's deer in China.

In England a British duke realized that European zoos had the only surviving Père David's deer. He bought them all—18 of them—and set them loose on his estate. After he died, his son and then his grandson took over their care.

In 1980 China approached the ducal family in England. Might they have some of their native deer back? After much discussion, a plan was approved and a suitable place chosen. Chinese workers planted grass and built a high wall around the parkland where the deer would be released. In 1986, for the first time in 86 years, 22 of China's native deer were back in China.

1. **Recognizing Words in Context**

   Find the word *hitherto* in the passage. One definition below is a *synonym* for that word; it means the same or almost the same thing. One definition is an *antonym*; it has the opposite or nearly opposite meaning. The other has a completely different meaning. Label the definitions S for *synonym*, A for *antonym*, and D for *different*.

   _____ a. subsequently
   _____ b. previously
   _____ c. pleasantly

2. **Distinguishing Fact from Opinion**

   Two of the statements below present *facts*, which can be proved correct. The other statement is an *opinion*, which expresses someone's thoughts or beliefs. Label the statements F for *fact* and O for *opinion*.

   _____ a. Twenty-two deer were returned to China in 1986.
   _____ b. Père David discovered the deer in 1865.
   _____ c. The deer were large and handsome.

3. Keeping Events in Order

Label the statements below 1, 2, and 3 to show the order in which the events happened.

_____ a. All the Père David's deer were shot during a rebellion in China in 1900.

_____ b. A British duke bought all the surviving deer in Europe and set them loose on his estate in England.

_____ c. Père David discovered large and handsome deer in China.

4. Making Correct Inferences

Two of the statements below are correct *inferences*, or reasonable guesses. They are based on information in the passage. The other statement is an incorrect, or faulty, inference. Label the statements C for *correct* inference and F for *faulty* inference.

_____ a. The British duke's actions saved the deer from extinction.

_____ b. The Chinese government did not care about the deer.

_____ c. The deer were special to the Chinese people.

5. Understanding Main Ideas

One of the statements below expresses the main idea of the passage. One statement is too general, or too broad. The other explains only part of the passage; it is too narrow. Label the statements M for *main idea*, B for *too broad*, and N for *too narrow.*

_____ a. A type of deer is returned to its native country.

_____ b. A British duke, realizing that Père David's deer were now extinct in China, bought the deer in Europe and set them loose on his property.

_____ c. After 86 years, China's native deer was returned to the Chinese people by the British family that saved the species.

Any device that is used to slow or stop a moving wheel or vehicle is called a brake. Brakes are also used in many cases to keep a stopped vehicle from moving. These devices work by transforming the energy of motion into heat. Most brakes utilize some friction in their operation. These are called friction brakes. They work by pressing a particular device against a moving part, such as a wheel rim.

The simplest form of friction brake is the mechanical brake. In the old-fashioned wagon brake, a lever is used to press a curved block against the rim of the rotating wagon wheel. The friction that is created slows and stops the wagon.

Another form of mechanical brake is the band brake. It works by means of a rope or flexible band that encircles a wheel or drum. When the band is tightened around the wheel or drum, it creates friction. Most band brakes are on the outside of drums, but some are fitted to expand on the inside, where the bands are protected from dirt. Band brakes are used in cranes, winches, and small engines. The earliest automobiles also used band brakes.

In modern automobiles, band brakes have been replaced by shoe brakes and disk brakes. The shoe brake uses two curved metal blocks called shoes that fit inside a drum attached to the wheel. The shoes push against the drum to stop the wheel. For disk brakes, the drum is replaced by one or more disks. Braking friction is created by friction pads or friction disks, which grasp the wheel's disks.

Mechanical brakes have levers or other mechanical linkages to help a person operate the brakes with less effort and more force. In automobiles and many other vehicles, hydraulic systems are often used in place of these mechanical linkages. Hydraulic brakes use water or a special brake fluid to transmit force from the person applying the brake to the working brake parts.

Compressed air is used in the operation of some brakes, especially on railroad trains. The Westinghouse compressed-air brake, for example, uses two compressed-air reservoirs. One is used in the normal operation of the brakes. Under normal conditions the air is released into a brake cylinder where it applies pressure that is transmitted to a brake shoe. In an accident, the second reservoir automatically releases its compressed air, forcing the brakes to stop the train.

Reading Time _____

Recalling Facts

1. Brakes work by transforming the energy of motion into
   - ❏ a. electricity.
   - ❏ b. force.
   - ❏ c. heat.

2. Most brakes operate by using
   - ❏ a. water.
   - ❏ b. friction.
   - ❏ c. compressed air.

3. Brakes that use water or special brake fluid are called
   - ❏ a. hydraulic brakes.
   - ❏ b. reservoir brakes.
   - ❏ c. pressure brakes.

4. The simplest form of friction brake is the
   - ❏ a. disk brake.
   - ❏ b. wagon brake.
   - ❏ c. mechanical brake.

5. Brakes found on railroad trains operate using
   - ❏ a. disks.
   - ❏ b. drums.
   - ❏ c. compressed air.

Understanding Ideas

6. You can conclude from the article that because band brakes are no longer used in automobiles,
   - ❏ a. other types of brakes are more effective.
   - ❏ b. band brakes are dangerous.
   - ❏ c. mechanical brakes should not be used in any vehicles.

7. The mechanical brake gets its name from
   - ❏ a. mechanical linkages used in that kind of system.
   - ❏ b. the routine operation of the brakes.
   - ❏ c. the Machine Age.

8. You can conclude from the article that brake selection is dependent on
   - ❏ a. how the brake will be used.
   - ❏ b. the cost of a brake system.
   - ❏ c. whether a vehicle is stopped or moving.

9. You can conclude from the article that compressed air brakes are especially effective on
   - ❏ a. airplanes.
   - ❏ b. automobiles.
   - ❏ c. railroad trains.

10. From the article you can conclude that a train's second compressed-air reservoir is automatically applied during an accident because
    - ❏ a. the first compressed-air reservoir brake automatically fails.
    - ❏ b. there may not be time to apply the first brake.
    - ❏ c. a train requires two sets of brakes to stop quickly.

5 B   Air Brakes

Richard Noble sat at the wheel of the Thrust 2 looking across the flat sands of Nevada's Black Rock Desert. Within moments he would fire the Rolls-Royce jet engine that powered his bullet-shaped vehicle. Would today be the day he broke the land speed record of 622 mph (1001.4 km/h) set by Gary Gabelich in 1970?

Speeds had increased greatly since Karl Benz's motor car chugged along at 9 mph (14.5 km/h) in 1886. Between 1924 and 1935, Sir Malcolm Campbell had broken the land speed record nine times! In 1964 Sir Malcolm's son Donald set a record of 403 mph (648.8 km/h). Noble knew that record was still standing for wheel-driven cars. Only jet-propelled vehicles had gone faster. Noble took a few deep breaths and readied himself for the challenge.

With a roar like a jet plane taking off, the Thrust 2 hurtled across the sand. Faster and faster it went until it was just a blur. Then parachutes blossomed from its tail. There was no way ordinary brakes could stop a vehicle going at that speed! The parachutes filled with air, dragging against the car's forward motion until it rolled to a stop. Cheers greeted Noble as he climbed out. He had set a new record of 633 mph (1,019.1 km/h)!

1. **Recognizing Words in Context**

   Find the word *fire* in the passage. One definition below is a *synonym* for that word; it means the same or almost the same thing. One definition is an *antonym*; it has the opposite or nearly opposite meaning. The other has a completely different meaning. Label the definitions S for *synonym*, A for *antonym*, and D for *different*.

   _____ a. shoot
   _____ b. stop
   _____ c. start

2. **Distinguishing Fact from Opinion**

   Two of the statements below present *facts*, which can be proved correct. The other statement is an *opinion*, which expresses someone's thoughts or beliefs. Label the statements F for *fact* and O for *opinion*.

   _____ a. Richard Noble is the fastest man on Earth.
   _____ b. Richard Noble's new record was 633 mph (1,019.1 km/h).
   _____ c. Sir Malcolm Campbell broke the land speed record nine times.

3. Keeping Events in Order

Two of the statements below describe events that happened at the same time. The other statement describes an event that happened before or after those events. Label them S for *same time,* B for *before,* and A for *after.*

_____ a. The vehicle's engine roared like a jet plane taking off.

_____ b. The Thrust 2 hurtled across the sand.

_____ c. Parachutes blossomed from the vehicle's tail.

4. Making Correct Inferences

Two of the statements below are correct *inferences,* or reasonable guesses. They are based on information in the passage. The other statement is an incorrect, or faulty, inference. Label the statements C for *correct* inference and F for *faulty* inference.

_____ a. Vehicle speeds have been steadily increasing over the years.

_____ b. No one has tried to break the land speed record for wheel-driven vehicles since 1964.

_____ c. Breaking records is important to drivers like Richard Noble.

5. Understanding Main Ideas

One of the statements below expresses the main idea of the passage. One statement is too general, or too broad. The other explains only part of the passage; it is too narrow. Label the statements M for *main idea,* B for *too broad,* and N for *too narrow.*

_____ a. The Thrust 2 was powered by a Rolls-Royce jet engine.

_____ b. Many people—men and women—have competed to be the fastest on land.

_____ c. Richard Noble set a new land speed record in a vehicle named Thrust 2.

Correct Answers, Part A _____

Correct Answers, Part B _____

Total Correct Answers _____

Dragons

According to a legend of the Middle Ages, there once lived in a distant pagan land a dreadful monster called a dragon. The flapping of its great wings could be heard for miles around. With a single blow of its terrible claws it could fell an ox. From the dragon's nostrils came clouds of smoke and flame that brought death to all who breathed it.

Every year a young girl was offered to the dragon to prevent it from rushing upon the city and destroying the inhabitants. One year the lot fell to Princess Sabra, daughter of the king. She was saved by the valiant St. George, youngest and bravest of the seven champions of Christendom.

With his magic sword Ascalon, he wounded the monster so badly that the princess was able to put her sash about its head and lead it to the marketplace of the town. There St. George slew it with one blow. Won over to the Christian faith by this deed of its champion, the people were baptized.

This is but one of many dragon stories in the folklore of different countries. Before the time of Columbus and the age of discovery, sailors refused to venture into unknown seas for fear of encountering dragons and other monsters of the deep. Old maps show the uncharted seas filled with strange creatures having wings, horns, and claws of such enormous size that they could crush a ship. The dragons of Chinese and Japanese myth and art were reptiles with batlike wings and claws. Such beasts were supposed to spread disease and death among the people. For ages the dragon was the emblem of the former imperial house of China.

These superstitions may have been based on the enormous reptiles that roamed the prehistoric world. Dinosaurs lived in the ages before humans appeared on Earth; however, some reptiles of great size may have existed at the time of the primitive cavemen of Europe. Such creatures could easily have given rise to legends of monsters such as dragons.

In the East Indies certain small lizards—no larger than a human hand— are known as dragons. They are the color of tree bark. The skin along their sides between the legs spreads out into a kind of parachute, enabling them to fly among the branches of the trees in which they live. There are about 20 species of these lizards, all harmless.

Reading Time _____

Recalling Facts

1. Dragon stories have been popular
   - ❏ a. since prehistoric time.
   - ❏ b. in the folklore of many countries.
   - ❏ c. mostly in China and Japan.

2. Dragon legends may have originated from
   - ❏ a. prehistoric reptiles.
   - ❏ b. lizards in the East Indies.
   - ❏ c. European bats.

3. The dragon is the emblem of
   - ❏ a. the former imperial house of China.
   - ❏ b. current Japanese royalty.
   - ❏ c. sailors.

4. Dinosaurs
   - ❏ a. predate humans on Earth.
   - ❏ b. appeared after humans.
   - ❏ c. are mythical creatures.

5. Certain small lizards in the East Indies are
   - ❏ a. brightly colored.
   - ❏ b. able to fly.
   - ❏ c. known as dinosaurs.

Understanding Ideas

6. From the article you can conclude that dragons of folklore inspired
   - ❏ a. worship.
   - ❏ b. fear.
   - ❏ c. laughter.

7. The article wants you to understand that stories about dragons are
   - ❏ a. factual.
   - ❏ b. folklore that may have a factual basis.
   - ❏ c. really stories about dinosaurs.

8. You can conclude from the article that after Columbus's time, sailors
   - ❏ a. refused to sail unknown seas.
   - ❏ b. killed many dragons at sea.
   - ❏ c. became less fearful of unknown seas.

9. Today dragons represent
   - ❏ a. folklore of the past.
   - ❏ b. creatures to be avoided.
   - ❏ c. fearful things in life.

10. Small, harmless lizards in the East Indies are called dragons, which is
    - ❏ a. practical.
    - ❏ b. untrue.
    - ❏ c. ironic.

The Komodo Dragon

On the Indonesian island of Komodo, dragons still roam the earth. Komodo dragons are giant lizards that can grow to be 10 feet (3 meters) long and can weigh up to 300 pounds (135 kilograms).

Komodo dragons hatch from eggs laid by the female in a burrow she digs. The eggs take about four months to hatch. As soon as the hatchlings emerge, they scramble up a nearby tree, where they stay, eating insects and smaller lizards, until they are about 4 feet (1.2 meters) long.

As they get older and heavier, the young dragons look for caves or dig burrows at the edge of the forest. When they come out to hunt, they lie in wait until a pig or a deer—their favorite food—wanders by, and then they strike. If they can catch smaller dragons, they will eat them. Komodo dragons will also look for and eat birds' eggs and dig up and eat the eggs of other lizards. Stories are also told of dragons capturing people, but there is no proof.

About 2,000 Komodo dragons still roam in the wild, but their habitat is shrinking because human population is increasing. Thousands of tourists arrive on Komodo each year just to see them. More than 200 are in zoo breeding programs aimed at keeping nature's only dragon from extinction.

1. Recognizing Words in Context

Find the word *hatchling* in the passage. One definition below is a *synonym* for that word; it means the same or almost the same thing. One definition is an *antonym*; it has the opposite or nearly opposite meaning. The other has a completely different meaning. Label the definitions S for *synonym*, A for *antonym*, and D for *different*.

_____ a. adult
_____ b. baby
_____ c. female

2. Distinguishing Fact from Opinion

Two of the statements below present *facts*, which can be proved correct. The other statement is an *opinion*, which expresses someone's thoughts or beliefs. Label the statements F for *fact* and O for *opinion*.

_____ a. Komodo dragons are giant lizards.
_____ b. Dragon eggs take about four months to hatch.
_____ c. The dragons' favorite food is pig or deer.

3. Keeping Events in Order

Label the statements below 1, 2, and 3 to show the order in which the events happened.

_____ a. Hatchling dragons live in trees.

_____ b. Young dragons look for caves in which to live.

_____ c. The female lays eggs in a burrow.

4. Making Correct Inferences

Two of the statements below are correct *inferences,* or reasonable guesses. They are based on information in the passage. The other statement is an incorrect, or faulty, inference. Label the statements C for *correct* inference and F for *faulty* inference.

_____ a. Komodo dragons may become endangered.

_____ b. Komodo dragons are mild tempered and not dangerous.

_____ c. Komodo dragons are one of nature's most unusual creatures.

5. Understanding Main Ideas

One of the statements below expresses the main idea of the passage. One statement is too general, or too broad. The other explains only part of the passage; it is too narrow. Label the statements M for *main idea,* B for *too broad,* and N for *too narrow.*

_____ a. Dragons really do exist.

_____ b. Komodo dragons live in caves or burrows and hunt by lying in wait for pigs and deer.

_____ c. Komodo dragons are giant hunting lizards of Indonesia.

Correct Answers, Part A _____

Correct Answers, Part B _____

Total Correct Answers _____

36

Open Wide

Dentists recommend that everyone have a dental checkup at least once a year. A dental examination includes X-rays of the teeth to detect decay or other problems, such as an impacted tooth. An impacted tooth is one that is unable to break through the gum. The condition of the gums and other soft tissue is also noted during routine checkups. Previous dental work, such as fillings, are examined for flaws that need correcting.

When a tooth is found to have a cavity, the decay is removed with a high-speed drill before the cavity can be filled. Usually, the area where the work is to be done is numbed first with a local anesthetic. The material used to fill the cavity may be a mixture of silver and mercury, or it may be gold, porcelain, or plastic. This is packed tightly into the cavity and the outer surface is smoothed.

When decay reaches the pulp of a tooth and inflames the nerve, causing pain and infection, root canal treatment is necessary. The pulp is removed from the tooth and replaced with metal, cement, or some other material. A crown, gold inlay, or filling material is used to close the cavity. Crowns, or caps, cover the entire tooth. These are used when the enamel of a tooth has been removed. Crowns are made of porcelain, plastic, or gold.

Pulling a tooth, or tooth extraction, is considered a last resort. Dentistry today strives to preserve the teeth and avoid dentures, if possible. Some exceptions to this rule improve the health of the mouth. An impacted wisdom tooth, or third molar, for example, can crowd the teeth and cause discomfort. Teeth may also be removed when the jawbone is too small to have room for all the teeth.

Dentures, either partial or complete, must be carefully fitted to the patient. Partial dentures, or bridgework, can be used when some of the natural teeth remain in the mouth. Such dentures may be removable; they are held in place by clasps that attach to nearby teeth. A fixed bridge is permanently attached to natural teeth. Complete dentures are removable and are held in place, if properly fitted, without adhesive pastes and powders.

Misaligned teeth can be slowly straightened with a structure of metal bands and wires, commonly known as braces. The best results are obtained when this treatment, called orthodontia, begins in childhood or adolescence.

Reading Time _____

Recalling Facts

1. Tooth problems can be discovered through
   - ❏ a. X-rays.
   - ❏ b. photographs.
   - ❏ c. sonar.

2. A tooth that is unable to break through the gums is referred to as
   - ❏ a. extracted.
   - ❏ b. decayed.
   - ❏ c. impacted.

3. When the enamel of a tooth is removed, the tooth is covered with a
   - ❏ a. crown.
   - ❏ b. hat.
   - ❏ c. sleeve.

4. The treatment for straightening teeth is called
   - ❏ a. surgery.
   - ❏ b. dentistry.
   - ❏ c. orthodontia.

5. The aim of dentistry is usually to
   - ❏ a. preserve teeth and avoid dentures.
   - ❏ b. extract teeth.
   - ❏ c. straighten teeth.

Understanding Ideas

6. From the article you can conclude that yearly dental checkups
   - ❏ a. help avoid serious problems.
   - ❏ b. are unnecessary.
   - ❏ c. prevent cavities.

7. Dentures are
   - ❏ a. a kind of braces.
   - ❏ b. natural teeth.
   - ❏ c. artificial teeth.

8. It is likely that an adult wearing braces
   - ❏ a. probably has dentures.
   - ❏ b. would have gotten better results from braces worn during childhood.
   - ❏ c. is wasting money.

9. A local anesthetic is used to
   - ❏ a. cause discomfort.
   - ❏ b. ease pain.
   - ❏ c. fight infection.

10. From the article you can conclude that people who visit dentists regularly
    - ❏ a. have healthy mouths.
    - ❏ b. are most likely to wear dentures.
    - ❏ c. have straight teeth.

Ancient Dentistry

The ancient Egyptians were pioneers in the field of dentistry. Bad teeth were common among Egyptians. The stone-ground bread they ate was full of sand and grit. This wore away the protective enamel of teeth and left them vulnerable to decay. The tomb of an Egyptian doctor who died some 5,000 years ago had on it the sign for "tooth." This suggests that his specialty was dentistry.

From around 700 B.C. Etruscan dentists were creating partial dentures, or bridgework. Some bridges could be removed for cleaning. Others were permanently attached to the surviving original teeth. Wide bands of gold fitted over the natural teeth. The fake tooth was held in place with a pin in one of the bands.

The Maya of Central America also used false teeth. In a human jawbone found in the region, pieces of shell replaced three teeth. The jawbone and primitive dentures are believed to belong to a Mayan who lived about A.D. 700.

In medieval China, fillings for cavities were available. A hardened paste of mercury, silver, and tin was used to fill the hole left by decay.

In ancient Rome, however, pulling teeth was the general practice. Barbers often performed this procedure. More than a hundred human teeth were found when a barbershop near the Roman Forum was excavated.

1. Recognizing Words in Context

Find the word *natural* in the passage. One definition below is a *synonym* for that word; it means the same or almost the same thing. One definition is an *antonym*; it has the opposite or nearly opposite meaning. The other has a completely different meaning. Label the definitions S for *synonym*, A for *antonym*, and D for *different*.

_____ a. artificial
_____ b. original
_____ c. inborn

2. Distinguishing Fact from Opinion

Two of the statements below present *facts*, which can be proved correct. The other statement is an *opinion*, which expresses someone's thoughts or beliefs. Label the statements F for *fact* and O for *opinion*.

_____ a. Dentistry doesn't seem to have improved much since ancient times.
_____ b. Bridgework has been around for more than 2,000 years.
_____ c. The ancient Romans pulled decayed teeth.

3. Keeping Events in Order

Label the statements below 1, 2, and 3 to show the order in which the events happened.

_____ a. The Maya used shells to create false teeth.

_____ b. The Etruscans created bridges made of gold bands.

_____ c. An Egyptian doctor had a sign meaning "tooth" inscribed on his tomb.

4. Making Correct Inferences

Two of the statements below are correct *inferences*, or reasonable guesses. They are based on information in the passage. The other statement is an incorrect, or faulty, inference. Label the statements C for *correct* inference and F for *faulty* inference.

_____ a. Dentistry is the most ancient of all professions.

_____ b. Bad teeth have been a human problem throughout history.

_____ c. People throughout history have been attempting to find ways to care for problems with teeth.

5. Understanding Main Ideas

One of the statements below expresses the main idea of the passage. One statement is too general, or too broad. The other explains only part of the passage; it is too narrow. Label the statements M for *main idea*, B for *too broad*, and N for *too narrow*.

_____ a. Dentistry has a history dating back to prehistoric times.

_____ b. As long ago as the days of ancient Egypt, dentists were trying to care for people's teeth.

_____ c. The Maya replaced teeth with pieces of shell.

Correct Answers, Part A _____

Correct Answers, Part B _____

Total Correct Answers _____

Unlike many animals, humans do not swim by instinct. Yet they can learn to swim better than almost any land animal. They need only master the proper strokes and ways of breathing.

A vital task in learning to swim is proper breathing. Swimmers inhale through the mouth and exhale through either the mouth or nose or both. Coaches often instruct pupils to inhale deeply and quickly but to exhale slowly. A swimmer can practice breathing by wading into waist-deep water, inhaling through the mouth and bending forward until the face is submerged. The swimmer then counts to 10 while holding the breath, lifts the head, and exhales. A swimmer can practice exhaling under water by keeping the eyes open and watching the bubbles. The swimmer then turns the face to one side and brings the mouth above the water to inhale.

A swimmer next learns to coast through the water. The swimmer wades into hip-deep water, faces the shore, and stoops down with arms extended beyond the head. The swimmer then shoves vigorously with the feet and floats as far as possible. To breathe, the swimmer pushes down with the hands, raises the head, and drops the feet to the bottom. A new swimmer should learn to coast 15 feet (4.5 meters) or so, exhaling under water. Swimmers who can do this are ready to learn the crawl, which is the fastest and most useful of all strokes.

When learning the crawl stroke, a swimmer floats on the stomach and kicks the legs slowly up and down. Toes should be turned inward and the knees held straight but relaxed. To move more quickly through the water, the swimmer kicks the legs in a rapid movement, called a flutter kick.

The arm movement for the crawl is an alternate reaching-out stroke. The arm is fully extended directly in front of the shoulder, palm down, and then brought straight down to the hip. One arm goes forward as the other comes back.

A swimmer breathes while doing the crawl by bending forward slightly, turning the face to one side and inhaling through the mouth during the recovery of the arm on the same side. The face is then turned down and the swimmer exhales under water. A swimmer can breathe from either side, whichever is more comfortable. Most swimmers prefer to breathe to their right side during the recovery of the right arm.

Reading Time _____

Recalling Facts

1. Humans who are excellent swimmers
   - ❏ a. have mastered the proper strokes and breathing.
   - ❏ b. swim by instinct.
   - ❏ c. practice every day.

2. The fastest and most useful swimming stroke is the
   - ❏ a. back stroke.
   - ❏ b. breast stroke.
   - ❏ c. crawl.

3. The crawl requires a swimmer to float on the
   - ❏ a. back.
   - ❏ b. stomach.
   - ❏ c. side.

4. The flutter kick is a
   - ❏ a. slow arm movement.
   - ❏ b. slow leg movement.
   - ❏ c. rapid leg movement.

5. When doing the crawl, swimmers breathe from
   - ❏ a. the left side.
   - ❏ b. the right side.
   - ❏ c. either side.

Understanding Ideas

6. Proper breathing while swimming
   - ❏ a. is the same as regular breathing.
   - ❏ b. is specialized and methodical.
   - ❏ c. is not very important.

7. The flutter kick works for a swimmer much like a boat's
   - ❏ a. motor.
   - ❏ b. oars.
   - ❏ c. wheel.

8. The arm movement for the crawl works much like a boat's
   - ❏ a. motor.
   - ❏ b. oars.
   - ❏ c. wheel.

9. The article suggests that learning to swim is best done
   - ❏ a. when a person is young.
   - ❏ b. in a pool.
   - ❏ c. in stages.

10. The article wants you to understand that
    - ❏ a. swimming is a learned skill.
    - ❏ b. some people are better swimmers than others.
    - ❏ c. swimming is an enjoyable sport.

Tim's Test

As a first-year lifeguard, Tim felt he had to prove himself to the other life-guards. Even though he had the same lifesaving certification as everyone else, he wanted to improve his swimming and rescue skills.

Every morning before the lifeguards' official duties began, Tim practiced swimming out beyond the breakers. He began by towing one float along with him, as every lifeguard did. Day by day, he added another and then another float. The added resistance these created caused him to work harder. Day by day, Tim's strength increased.

Lifeguards from all the town beaches competed in an annual tournament held in the middle of the summer. Tim was nervous about participating but excited at the thought of having a chance to prove himself. He entered the one-person lifesaving event.

At the signal, Tim plunged into the surf. With strong, sure strokes, he swam toward the drowning "victim"—another lifeguard who was playing the part and waiting for rescue. Tim reached his victim, secured him safely, and swam rapidly back to shore. As he pulled the victim onto shore, a swift glance showed that he was the first competitor to reach land. His team-mates surrounded him, cheering. Tim had won the race and the respect of his fellow lifeguards.

1. Recognizing Words in Context

Find the word *swift* in the passage. One definition below is a *synonym* for that word; it means the same or almost the same thing. One definition is an *antonym*; it has the opposite or nearly opposite meaning. The other has a completely different meaning. Label the definitions S for *synonym*, A for *antonym,* and D for *different.*

_____ a. rapid
_____ b. slow
_____ c. unnecessary

2. Distinguishing Fact from Opinion

Two of the statements below present *facts*, which can be proved correct. The other statement is an *opinion,* which expresses someone's thoughts or beliefs. Label the statements F for *fact* and O for *opinion.*

_____ a. Tim wanted to earn the approval of his fellow lifeguards.
_____ b. Tim's skills improved to the point where he won a contest.
_____ c. Tim was the best swimmer among all the town's lifeguards.

3. Keeping Events in Order

Label the statements below 1, 2, and 3 to show the order in which the events happened.

_____ a. Tim worked on his swimming and rescue skills every morning.

_____ b. Tim was the first competitor to reach land.

_____ c. At the signal, Tim plunged into the surf.

4. Making Correct Inferences

Two of the statements below are correct *inferences,* or reasonable guesses. They are based on information in the passage. The other statement is an incorrect, or faulty, inference. Label the statements C for *correct* inference and F for *faulty* inference.

_____ a. Tim was a hardworking, dedicated lifeguard.

_____ b. Tim's efforts to improve his swimming and rescue skills were the reason he succeeded in the competition.

_____ c. Tim's teammates liked him only because he was successful in the race.

5. Understanding Main Ideas

One of the statements below expresses the main idea of the passage. One statement is too general, or too broad. The other explains only part of the passage; it is too narrow. Label the statements M for *main idea,* B for *too broad,* and N for *too narrow.*

_____ a. A lifeguard must be skilled in a variety of swimming and rescue techniques.

_____ b. Tim entered an event in an annual lifeguard tournament.

_____ c. Tim, a first-year lifeguard, worked hard to improve his swimming and rescue skills.

Correct Answers, Part A _____

Correct Answers, Part B _____

Total Correct Answers _____

At Home in the Zoo

Nearly every child and adult enjoys the zoo, but how about the animals? Many people wonder if it is cruel to remove animals from their homes and confine them behind bars and trenches where thousands of human beings stare at them.

In certain ways animals may fare better in zoos than in their natural surroundings. Wild animals may be underfed. Some must roam far and wide to find sufficient food. Some wild animals suffer from wounds or disease. Most animals must be on guard constantly against enemies. After a few weeks in a zoo, the steady food supply, clean living quarters, and medical care often give rise to an improvement in the physical health and appearance of captive animals. Many mate and rear young in captivity. Many also seem to enjoy human visitors just as much as the visitors enjoy them.

Bears and seals, for example, love to show off for zoo visitors. Monkeys and apes also appear to enjoy human companionship, especially that of their keepers. The Lincoln Park Zoo in Chicago once tried using one-way glass in the monkey house. People could look in and see the monkeys, but the monkeys could not look out and see the people. The monkeys became unhappy, and the glass was removed. At once, the animals regained their lively spirits.

Visitors may mistake certain animal actions as signs of unhappiness. Endless pacing back and forth may be simply an animal's way of getting exercise. When brown bears pad the ground for hours, they are following an instinct to pack down snow, even though they have no snow to pack. If a monkey gazes longingly into space, is it wishing it was back in the jungle? It is probably just waiting for its food.

Most animals have a great need to feel secure. They want an area to claim as their territory, a place where they can hide and feel safe. On the rare occasions when an animal escapes from a zoo, it usually comes back to its quarters after a few hours or days, especially if it escapes into areas of human habitation. That world—so different from the animal's native habitat and from its zoo quarters—is likely terrifying. The animal returns to the place where it feels secure and where it can find food and water. Often the animals walk back through the open cage door of their own accord.

Reading Time _____

Recalling Facts

1. Animals in the wild
   - ❏ a. are better fed than animals in zoos.
   - ❏ b. are often without sufficient food.
   - ❏ c. are well fed.

2. Animals in captivity
   - ❏ a. never mate.
   - ❏ b. may mate and rear young.
   - ❏ c. must often fight to protect themselves.

3. Most animals have a great need for
   - ❏ a. security.
   - ❏ b. isolation.
   - ❏ c. freedom.

4. Living in the wild is dangerous for animals because of
   - ❏ a. natural enemies.
   - ❏ b. bad weather.
   - ❏ c. lack of shelter.

5. Animals that like to show off include
   - ❏ a. lions.
   - ❏ b. crocodiles.
   - ❏ c. seals.

Understanding Ideas

6. From the article you can conclude that animals in zoos
   - ❏ a. are healthier than animals in the wild.
   - ❏ b. miss their natural surroundings.
   - ❏ c. dislike being caged.

7. Monkeys placed behind one-way glass were unhappy, which suggests that monkeys
   - ❏ a. like their privacy.
   - ❏ b. are social creatures.
   - ❏ c. are afraid of glass.

8. According to the article, animal instinct
   - ❏ a. disappears in captive animals.
   - ❏ b. remains strong in captive animals.
   - ❏ c. is stronger in wild animals.

9. From the article you can conclude that animals
   - ❏ a. imitate human behavior.
   - ❏ b. behave according to instinct.
   - ❏ c. change their behavior in a zoo environment.

10. The article suggests that concern about the well-being of captive animals is
    - ❏ a. justified.
    - ❏ b. exaggerated.
    - ❏ c. not based on fact.

9　B　　　Pachyderm Picasso

A recent book, *Why Cats Paint,* was a funny spoof that fooled people with its photographs of cats "painting." Cats may not really paint, but other animals do. Ruby, an 8,000-pound Asian elephant at the Phoenix Zoo, is perhaps the best-known animal artist. Her paintings sell for $1,000 or more and hang in private collections beside the works of famous human artists.

How did Ruby's keepers get the idea of letting her paint? Elephants have been observed using their trunks to draw in the dirt and marking the ground with twigs or rocks. Ruby had always doodled like this, so her keepers decided to give her art lessons and materials. Within a week, Ruby was painting like a pro.

Ruby is given a canvas and several choices of brushes and paints. An elephant's trunk contains 50,000 different muscles and can weigh as much as a man, but it can hold a paintbrush and use it delicately. With the tip of her trunk, Ruby points to the brush and the color she wants. Her keeper dips the brush in the color of her choice and hands it to her. When a keeper tries to give her a color she has not selected, she refuses to use it.

Where does an elephant get her ideas? Her keepers think that the red and blue that dominate one of Ruby's best-known works, "Fire Truck," might have been inspired by emergency vehicles that arrived at the zoo to rescue a man who had collapsed.

1. Recognizing Words in Context

Find the word *different* in the passage. One definition below is a *synonym* for that word; it means the same or almost the same thing. One definition is an *antonym*; it has the opposite or nearly opposite meaning. The other has a completely different meaning. Label the definitions S for *synonym*, A for *antonym*, and D for *different*.

_____ a. unusual
_____ b. identical
_____ c. separate

2. Distinguishing Fact from Opinion

Two of the statements below present *facts*, which can be proved correct. The other statement is an *opinion*, which expresses someone's thoughts or beliefs. Label the statements F for *fact* and O for *opinion*.

_____ a. It's amazing to think of an elephant painting.
_____ b. Ruby's paintings hang beside the works of famous human artists.
_____ c. When offered a color she has not selected, Ruby will refuse to use it.

3. Keeping Events in Order

Label the statements below 1, 2, and 3 to show the order in which the events happened.

_____ a. The keeper hands Ruby a brush with paint on it.

_____ b. Ruby is given a canvas and a choice of brushes and paints.

_____ c. Ruby uses the tip of her trunk to indicate the brush and color she wants to use.

4. Making Correct Inferences

Two of the statements below are correct *inferences*, or reasonable guesses. They are based on information in the passage. The other statement is an incorrect, or faulty, inference. Label the statements C for *correct* inference and F for *faulty* inference.

_____ a. Ruby has definite ideas about the colors she wants to use in a painting.

_____ b. Ruby's keepers knew that given a chance, she would be a talented artist.

_____ c. An elephant's trunk is a useful tool.

5. Understanding Main Ideas

One of the statements below expresses the main idea of the passage. One statement is too general, or too broad. The other explains only part of the passage; it is too narrow. Label the statements M for *main idea*, B for *too broad*, and N for *too narrow*.

_____ a. An elephant's trunk contains 50,000 different muscles.

_____ b. Ruby, an Asian elephant, is an animal artist whose paintings hang in collections with the works of famous human artists.

_____ c. A variety of animals, including elephants, have been known to use paint creatively.

Correct Answers, Part A _____

Correct Answers, Part B _____

Total Correct Answers _____

The Oracle at Delphi

In ancient Greece, the people turned to their gods for answers to questions, for advice about problems that worried them. Both the god's answer and the shrine where worshipers sought the god's advice were called an oracle. The most celebrated oracle was at Delphi on the south slope of Mount Parnassus. Here a sacred stone supposedly marked the exact center of the Earth. Nearby flowed the sacred fountain of Castalia. Over the centuries, several temples were built at Delphi to Apollo. Apollo was revered as the god of light, poetry and music, and prophecy. People came from every part of Greece to learn the future through the wisdom of Apollo as revealed in the oracles.

In ancient days there was a crack in the ground at Delphi. From it came volcanic vapors said to possess strange powers. A priestess, called the Pythia, sat on a tripod placed over this vent. After first bathing in a sacred stream and eating the leaves of the sacred laurel, she breathed the vapors and went into a trance. Her weird sounds and chants were taken down by priests and put into verse. They were presented as the words of Apollo to those who came seeking advice. These oracles were worded to suggest more than one meaning.

Everyone who asked advice at Delphi was expected to bring gifts. Great treasuries were built to hold the offerings presented by rulers, states, and individuals. Many gifts were of pure gold or silver. Enemies who conquered Greece looted these treasuries. Nero, the Roman emperor, is said to have stolen 500 statues. Even so, it was reported that 3,000 still remained. Modern excavations have uncovered temple ruins, pieces of sculpture, and historic inscriptions.

Before any important step was taken in affairs of state, the oracle at Delphi was consulted. It thus exerted a powerful influence on the history of the Greeks. The oracle's words were revered and treasured. Festivals and games were held near the shrine every four years. These observances promoted unity in the political and religious life of the Greek world.

The oracle at Delphi was the most famous, but it was only one of several Greek oracles. The oldest was that of Zeus at Dodona, in Epirus. Here Zeus was believed to speak through the rustling of the leaves of the sacred oak tree. There were also oracles in Rome and in Egypt, Babylonia, and other countries.

Reading Time _____

Recalling Facts

1. Ancient Greeks believed that a stone on Mount Parnassus marked
   - ❑ a. the end of the Earth.
   - ❑ b. the center of the Earth.
   - ❑ c. a sacred burial ground.

2. An oracle is both a shrine to a god and
   - ❑ a. the god's answer to a question.
   - ❑ b. a priestess on a tripod.
   - ❑ c. a riddle for a king.

3. The most celebrated oracle was located in
   - ❑ a. Rome.
   - ❑ b. Delphi.
   - ❑ c. Egypt.

4. Apollo was the Greek god of light, poetry and music, and
   - ❑ a. farming.
   - ❑ b. beauty.
   - ❑ c. prophecy.

5. Greeks believed that Zeus spoke through the
   - ❑ a. chirping of birds.
   - ❑ b. rustling of leaves.
   - ❑ c. roar of the ocean.

Understanding Ideas

6. Ancient Greeks could be considered
   - ❑ a. very religious.
   - ❑ b. moderately religious.
   - ❑ c. not religious.

7. It is likely that before making a political decision, a Greek leader would
   - ❑ a. visit the oracle at Delphi.
   - ❑ b. ask a priest for help.
   - ❑ c. make an offering to Nero.

8. From the article you can conclude that the influence of priests was
   - ❑ a. minor.
   - ❑ b. major.
   - ❑ c. nonexistent.

9. From the article you can conclude that Nero, the Roman emperor, was
   - ❑ a. a friend of Greece.
   - ❑ b. an enemy of Greece.
   - ❑ c. conquered by Greece.

10. It is likely that modern excavations in Greece
    - ❑ a. have located all the treasuries holding gifts.
    - ❑ b. will continue to search for treasures.
    - ❑ c. will cease.

10   B   Consulting the Oracle

Throughout the known world, King Croesus, ruler of Lydia in Asia Minor was famous for his great wealth. He had conquered almost all the nations that surrounded his, yet Croesus still was not satisfied. He dreamed of conquering the great Persian Empire.

Before taking action against the Persians, Croesus wanted to be certain he would succeed. He decided to consult the oracle at Delphi. To win the favor of the god Apollo, Croesus sacrificed thousands of animals and sent many gifts of gold and silver to the oracle. Croesus commanded the men he sent to the oracle with these gifts to ask whether he should undertake a war against the Persians. They returned with the oracle's answer: "If you make war on the Persians, you will destroy a great empire."

Croesus was overjoyed with this answer. He sent more gifts to thank the oracle. Then he marched on Persia with his army.

Following a battle that neither side won, Croesus fell back to the city of Sardis. He hoped to call on his Egyptian allies for help. However, after a 14-day siege, Sardis fell to the Persians, and Croesus was captured. The great empire that the oracle had predicted Croesus would destroy was his own.

1. Recognizing Words in Context

Find the word *ruler* in the passage. One definition below is a *synonym* for that word; it means the same or almost the same thing. One definition is an *antonym*; it has the opposite or nearly opposite meaning. The other has a completely different meaning. Label the definitions S for *synonym*, A for *antonym*, and D for *different*.

_____ a. measuring stick
_____ b. follower
_____ c. leader

2. Distinguishing Fact from Opinion

Two of the statements below present *facts*, which can be proved correct. The other statement is an *opinion*, which expresses someone's thoughts or beliefs. Label the statements F for *fact* and O for *opinion*.

_____ a. King Croesus was famous for his great wealth.
_____ b. Croesus asked the Delphic oracle whether he should attack the Persian Empire.
_____ c. Croesus was a greedy and foolish man.

3. Keeping Events in Order

Label the statements below 1, 2, and 3 to show the order in which the events happened.

_____ a. The oracle said that Croesus would destroy a great empire.

_____ b. The Persians defeated Croesus at Sardis.

_____ c. Croesus sent men to ask the oracle whether he should attack the Persians.

4. Making Correct Inferences

Two of the statements below are correct *inferences,* or reasonable guesses. They are based on information in the passage. The other statement is an incorrect, or faulty, inference. Label the statements C for *correct* inference and F for *faulty* inference.

_____ a. The Persian forces were stronger than those of the Lydians.

_____ b. The oracle's predictions always came true.

_____ c. The oracle's answers to questions were worded so that they could be interpreted in more than one way.

5. Understanding Main Ideas

One of the statements below expresses the main idea of the passage. One statement is too general, or too broad. The other explains only part of the passage; it is too narrow. Label the statements M for *main idea,* B for *too broad,* and N for *too narrow.*

_____ a. Because of an oracle's prediction, King Croesus of Lydia attacked the Persian Empire and was defeated.

_____ b. Rulers of nations, wealthy individuals, and other people believed in the predictions made by the Delphic oracle.

_____ c. The oracle at Delphi told Croesus he would destroy a great empire if he made war on the Persians.

Correct Answers, Part A _____

Correct Answers, Part B _____

Total Correct Answers _____

The dream of flight is perhaps as old as humanity. Although most modern flight is for commercial or military purposes, the early pioneers of aviation wanted to fly just for the thrill of it. Today, people worldwide enjoy that thrill in a variety of aerial sports. These sports may use powered planes, lighter-than-air balloons, gliders, parachutes, or hang gliders. Hang gliding has become one of the most popular sports today. Also known as soaring, hang gliding is said to be the nearest possible way for a human to feel like a bird in flight.

A hang glider consists of a fabric wing attached to a lightweight, portable frame. The wings are usually made of Dacron, a fabric that can withstand great stress. A typical hang glider wing is about 32 feet (9.8 meters) long and 7 feet (2.1 meters) wide. Aluminum tubing braces the structure. The pilot hangs beneath the wing in a harness and grips a horizontal control bar. The entire hang glider weighs only about 40 to 70 pounds (88.2 to 154.3 kilograms).

A hang-glider pilot often takes off by running downhill into the wind or a thermal—a rising air current. Skilled fliers may take off from a cliff, but that method is dangerous and difficult. In the air, the pilot moves his or her body and the control bar to change the glider's center of gravity. These changes cause the glider to turn or to go up or down. Like regular glider pilots, the hang-glider pilot uses thermals to gain altitude and maintain it.

Otto Lilienthal of Germany experimented with hang gliders as well as regular gliders in the late 1800s. Few others, however, showed much interest in them until 1951. That year, U.S. space scientist Francis Rogallo and his wife, Gertrude, patented their "flexible kite." This kite had no sticks, and its frame was flexible rather than rigid. The flexible kite developed into the first modern hang glider later in the 1950s. Today, one of the most popular and easily flown models is called the Rogallo wing, which is about 18 feet (5.5 meters) long and weighs about 35 pounds (77.2 kilograms).

Hang gliding became especially popular in California and Australia during the 1960s. Competition in the sport has been growing rapidly since the early 1970s. Most events test the pilots' form and skill in distance runs, target landings, banked turns, and full-circle turns.

Reading Time _____

Recalling Facts

1. Otto Lilienthal of Germany
   - ❏ a. invented the hang glider.
   - ❏ b. was the first person to use a hang glider.
   - ❏ c. experimented with hang gliders.

2. The first modern hang glider developed from
   - ❏ a. Lilienthal's glider experiments.
   - ❏ b. Rogallo's flexible kite.
   - ❏ c. the Rogallo wing.

3. Hang gliding is also known as
   - ❏ a. wind-sailing.
   - ❏ b. paragliding.
   - ❏ c. soaring.

4. A hang glider is partly controlled by moving a
   - ❏ a. vertical bar.
   - ❏ b. steering wheel.
   - ❏ c. horizontal bar.

5. Glider pilots gain and maintain altitude by
   - ❏ a. using thermals.
   - ❏ b. running downhill.
   - ❏ c. tipping the wing.

Understanding Ideas

6. From the article you can conclude that a pilot usually
   - ❏ a. weighs more than the hang glider.
   - ❏ b. weighs less than the hang glider.
   - ❏ c. weighs exactly the same as the hang glider.

7. From the article you can conclude that hang gliding
   - ❏ a. requires training.
   - ❏ b. is an easy sport to learn.
   - ❏ c. will soon become the most popular sport in the world.

8. From the article you can conclude that hang glider wings must be made of strong material because
   - ❏ a. they need to resist tearing if the glider crashes.
   - ❏ b. they must be able to withstand the force of strong air currents.
   - ❏ c. they might rip if the pilot is too heavy.

9. You can conclude from the article that a hang glider pilot makes a left turn by
   - ❏ a. moving his or her body to the left of center.
   - ❏ b. moving his or her body to the right of center.
   - ❏ c. finding a rising thermal.

10. The article suggests that people are attracted to aerial sports because
    - ❏ a. there is fierce competition.
    - ❏ b. they can make money.
    - ❏ c. they want to experience the thrill of flying.

High above the California desert, Kerri Hannum stood on a cliff edge under the bright pink wings of her hang glider. A moment later, she launched herself off the cliff, aiming for a thermal—a rising column of hot air. She hit it just right. All at once she was rising faster than 1,000 feet (304.8 meters) a minute! At 14,000 feet (4,267.2 meters) above the desert floor, she angled out of the thermal.

Suddenly, her breath was knocked out of her as a blast of heavy, cold air struck her. It bashed her downward with more force than she had ever encountered. Kerri fought to hold her glider steady. It was no use: the glider's nose was knocked from a three-o'clock position—level flight— through six o'clock—full dive. This had happened to Kerri before. Glider pilots called it "going over the falls." This time, however, Kerri's glider was shoved so hard that it pivoted on to nine o'clock—completely upside down! She was in danger of falling onto her glider and breaking its delicate structure of tubing and wires.

As Kerri pulled hard on the control bar to shift her weight forward and gain airspeed, her glider sank back into a controllable dive. She breathed a sigh of relief as she soared on.

1. Recognizing Words in Context

Find the word *hard* in the passage. One definition below is a *synonym* for that word; it means the same or almost the same thing. One definition is an *antonym*; it has the opposite or nearly opposite meaning. The other has a completely different meaning. Label the definitions S for *synonym*, A for *antonym*, and D for *different*.

_____ a. firm
_____ b. weakly
_____ c. strongly

2. Distinguishing Fact from Opinion

Two of the statements below present *facts*, which can be proved correct. The other statement is an *opinion*, which expresses someone's thoughts or beliefs. Label the statements F for *fact* and O for *opinion*.

_____ a. A thermal is a rising current of hot air.
_____ b. Thermals can carry hang gliders upward at more than 1,000 feet a minute.
_____ c. Anyone who hang-glides is foolhardy.

3. Keeping Events in Order

Two of the statements below describe events that happened at the same time. The other statement describes an event that happened before or after those events. Label them S for *same time*, B for *before*, and A for *after*.

_____ a. Kerri angled out of the thermal.

_____ b. A blast of heavy, cold air struck her.

_____ c. Kerri's glider went into a full dive.

4. Making Correct Inferences

Two of the statements below are correct *inferences*, or reasonable guesses. They are based on information in the passage. The other statement is an incorrect, or faulty, inference. Label the statements C for *correct* inference and F for *faulty* inference.

_____ a. Kerri Hannum is an experienced hang glider pilot.

_____ b. Hang gliders depend on rising currents of air to carry them up.

_____ c. Kerri Hannum should not have been hang gliding that day.

5. Understanding Main Ideas

One of the statements below expresses the main idea of the passage. One statement is too general, or too broad. The other explains only part of the passage; it is too narrow. Label the statements M for *main idea*, B for *too broad*, and N for *too narrow*.

_____ a. Hang glider pilot Kerri Hannum had a close call over the California desert.

_____ b. Hang glider pilots must learn to judge the different air currents they will encounter.

_____ c. A rising current of hot air carried Kerri's hang glider to 14,000 feet.

Correct Answers, Part A _____

Correct Answers, Part B _____

Total Correct Answers _____

The Worst of Pests

The cockroach is one of the most obnoxious of household pests. This brown or black insect can be found in houses, apartment and office buildings, ships, trains, and airplanes in many parts of the world. Domestic cockroaches, which are also called roaches, have a disagreeable odor. They live in warm, dark areas. Their broad, flat bodies permit them to crawl in narrow cracks and along pipes. They hide in the daytime, coming out at night to feed. The diet of the cockroach, which includes both plant and animal products, ranges from food, paper, clothing, and books to dead insects. Cockroaches can be difficult to eliminate entirely, but a variety of common poisons and traps are effective in controlling their numbers. They are thought to transmit several human diseases.

Cockroaches are among the oldest living insects. Fossil cockroaches that resemble today's species have been found in Coal Age deposits more than 320 million years old. About 3,500 species have been identified. Although the most pesky are those that infest households in the temperate regions, most species are tropical. Some reach lengths of several inches, and many are colorful. Several species of woodland cockroaches are found in temperate regions. These live amid decaying wood and other vegetation and do not enter houses.

The cockroach has long, powerful legs and can run very fast. Long antennae on the head are used for feeling in dark places. Most species have two pairs of wings that are larger in the males. The female cockroach carries her eggs in a leathery capsule at the rear of the abdomen. Females of some common species lay 16 to 45 eggs at a time. The eggs take from 4 to 12 weeks to hatch. After the female deposits the eggs, soft, white young called nymphs emerge. After exposure to air, the nymphs harden and turn brown.

The German cockroach is a common household pest. It is light brown with two dark stripes just behind the head. Because it is only about half an inch (12.7 millimeters) long, it can easily enter or be transported into homes.

The American cockroach, also called a waterbug, is long, reddish brown, and lives outdoors or in dark, heated indoor areas. Favorite places are basements and furnace rooms. This cockroach, a native of tropical and subtropical America, has well-developed wings and can fly long distances. Cockroaches are closely related to grasshoppers, katydids, and crickets.

Reading Time _____

Recalling Facts

1. Roaches live in areas that are
   - ❏ a. damp.
   - ❏ b. warm and dark.
   - ❏ c. cold.

2. The cockroach's long antennae on the head are used for
   - ❏ a. feeding.
   - ❏ b. feeling in dark places.
   - ❏ c. flying.

3. Young cockroaches are called
   - ❏ a. waterbugs.
   - ❏ b. fossils.
   - ❏ c. nymphs.

4. Young cockroaches harden and turn brown when they
   - ❏ a. hatch.
   - ❏ b. are exposed to air.
   - ❏ c. mature.

5. Cockroaches feed
   - ❏ a. at night.
   - ❏ b. during the day.
   - ❏ c. every two days.

Understanding Ideas

6. Cockroaches would most likely prefer living
   - ❏ a. near an oven.
   - ❏ b. in a warm, sunny spot.
   - ❏ c. by the ocean.

7. The cockroach's diet is best described as
   - ❏ a. limited.
   - ❏ b. wide-ranging.
   - ❏ c. meat-eating.

8. One reason that cockroaches are difficult to eliminate entirely might be that
   - ❏ a. there are many different species.
   - ❏ b. they can run very fast.
   - ❏ c. they can fly long distances.

9. Humans should beware cockroaches mainly because
   - ❏ a. they transmit diseases.
   - ❏ b. of their odor.
   - ❏ c. they devour human food.

10. Cockroaches have survived for millions of years, which suggests that they
    - ❏ a. live a long time.
    - ❏ b. are able to adapt to changing environments.
    - ❏ c. are decreasing in number.

The Eternal Cockroach

An ancient cockroach sat on a patch of moss in the dim red light of a dying sun. A young cockroach came to sit beside the old one. "Tell me about the dinosaurs, Grandfather," the young cockroach said.

"The dinosaurs were gigantic creatures!" the old one said. "The ground shook when they walked. Their voices were like thunder. They ruled the earth for millions of years. They never noticed us. We crept around and lived our quiet lives."

"What happened to them, Grandfather?" the young cockroach asked.

"Oh, they died out," the old one said. "And we didn't miss them when they were gone."

"Tell me about people, Grandfather," the young cockroach said next.

"People were big creatures," the old one said. "There were many, many of them. They filled the planet with their machines and their cities and their noise. They hated us and tried to kill us off with poisons and traps."

"What happened to them, Grandfather?" the young cockroach asked.

"Oh, they died out," the old one said. "And we didn't miss them when they were gone."

1. Recognizing Words in Context

Find the word *miss* in the passage. One definition below is a *synonym* for that word; it means the same or almost the same thing. One definition is an *antonym*; it has the opposite or nearly opposite meaning. The other has a completely different meaning. Label the definitions S for *synonym*, A for *antonym*, and D for *different*.

_____ a. disregard

_____ b. want

_____ c. fail

2. Distinguishing Fact from Opinion

Two of the statements below present *facts*, which can be proved correct. The other statement is an *opinion*, which expresses someone's thoughts or beliefs. Label the statements F for *fact* and O for *opinion*.

_____ a. Dinosaurs were gigantic creatures.

_____ b. People tried to kill cockroaches.

_____ c. Cockroaches did not care about dinosaurs or people.

3. Keeping Events in Order

Label the statements below 1, 2, and 3 to show the order in which the events happened.

_____ a. The old cockroach said that roaches didn't miss people when they were gone.

_____ b. The young cockroach asked the old one about the dinosaurs.

_____ c. The young cockroach asked the old one about people.

4. Making Correct Inferences

Two of the statements below are correct *inferences,* or reasonable guesses. They are based on information in the passage. The other statement is an incorrect, or faulty, inference. Label the statements C for *correct* inference and F for *faulty* inference.

_____ a. Cockroaches have an extremely long life span.

_____ b. This story takes place in the distant future.

_____ c. Cockroaches lived during the days of the dinosaurs.

5. Understanding Main Ideas

One of the statements below expresses the main idea of the passage. One statement is too general, or too broad. The other explains only part of the passage; it is too narrow. Label the statements M for *main idea,* B for *too broad,* and N for *too narrow.*

_____ a. Cockroaches are among the most ancient of Earth's creatures.

_____ b. Cockroaches, which lived during the days of the dinosaurs, will probably outlive human beings, too.

_____ c. The dinosaurs died out.

Correct Answers, Part A _____

Correct Answers, Part B _____

Total Correct Answers _____

13 A Technology: Is It Art?

At one time the same meaning was given to *art* that was applied to *technology*. Each was described as involving the use of skill to make or do something. Today, that blanket description is no longer true or accepted.

Technology is now generally thought of as applied science. The old definition does, however, still retain some validity. It addresses the role that skill plays in technology as well as in art. An artist's skill rests upon knowledge and experience. So does a technician's. The difference seems to lie in the creative application of the skill. The old definition also explains that technicians—like artists—transform matter. A sculptor may shape a block of marble into a statue. A technician may use a machine to combine silicon, metal, and plastic into a microchip.

Otherwise, art and technology have diverged. The goal of artists is to give permanence to the present—to speak to their age by creating works that will endure forever. The goal of technicians is to press on to the future and to new discoveries. Technology suggests permanent change and improvement. Once a new technique is developed and adopted, society does not attempt to revert to the former technique. The automobile replaced the horse and buggy; the electric light replaced kerosene lamps; sound movies replaced silent films; and word processors have made typewriters obsolete.

This forward march of technology is called progress. In the fine arts this type of progress does not exist. Today, for example, one can admire a Roman chariot, but few people would want to depend on it for transportation. By contrast, people are still astounded by the magnificence of Michelangelo's frescoes in the Vatican's Sistine Chapel. These paintings have an excellence that will never become outmoded.

In the late 20th century, art and technology have been somewhat reunited by the computer. Musical compositions can be created on a computer. It is also common to design three-dimensional models of commercial products or to sketch out blueprints using computer programs. Sculptors, filmmakers, architects, printmakers, and other workers in the visual arts increasingly use computers. It is even possible to create finished works of fine art on a computer screen. Still, the distinction between technology and art persists. Computers make the execution of some kinds of art more challenging and interesting; but they do not make the art of the present better than the art of the past.

Reading Time _____

Recalling Facts

1. The goal of technology is to
   - ❏ a. make new discoveries.
   - ❏ b. create beauty.
   - ❏ c. challenge artists.

2. Art is considered
   - ❏ a. an applied science.
   - ❏ b. a creative process.
   - ❏ c. a means to achieve progress.

3. Society regards technological changes as
   - ❏ a. advances.
   - ❏ b. negative reversals.
   - ❏ c. worthless.

4. The goal of artists is to
   - ❏ a. give permanence to the present.
   - ❏ b. make new discoveries.
   - ❏ c. outdo technology.

5. Creating musical compositions on a computer
   - ❏ a. has been possible since Michelangelo's time.
   - ❏ b. has recently been made possible.
   - ❏ c. is not possible.

Understanding Ideas

6. From the article you can conclude that Michelangelo was a great
   - ❏ a. artist.
   - ❏ b. Roman statesman.
   - ❏ c. minister.

7. Progress is a goal
   - ❏ a. for both art and technology.
   - ❏ b. more suitable to technology than to art.
   - ❏ c. more suitable to art than to technology.

8. The article suggests that computers
   - ❏ a. are useful tools for artists.
   - ❏ b. have made art more creative.
   - ❏ c. have had a negative effect on art.

9. From the article you can conclude that computers are used
   - ❏ a. primarily by technicians.
   - ❏ b. primarily by artists.
   - ❏ c. by artists and technicians alike.

10. The article wants you to understand that
    - ❏ a. technology is not art.
    - ❏ b. technology and art are the same thing.
    - ❏ c. art is impossible without technology.

Natasha spent weeks working on an oil painting. She applied layers of color, then waited for the paint to dry before adding more layers of color. Under her brush, a peaceful woodland scene slowly grew. Finally she put the last touches of paint on the canvas and set down her brush.

While Natasha put the finishing touches on her painting, her brother Andrew sat in front of a computer screen. Using his computer's painting tools, he chose line widths and brush strokes. He selected colors and shades. With movements and clicks of Andrew's mouse, a stormy ocean scene quickly grew. With a tap of his finger, Andrew sent the image to his printer.

"What do you think, Mom?" Natasha proudly presented her painting to her mother.

"How about my artwork, Mom?" Andrew held up the color printout of his creation.

"My painting took weeks!" said Natasha. "His took just a couple of hours. You can't call that art!"

"I think you're both terrific artists," their mother said diplomatically. "It doesn't matter how long it took or what tools you used. You've both expressed your emotions and your ideas in your work, and that's what makes it art."

1. Recognizing Words in Context

Find the word *creation* in the passage. One definition below is a *synonym* for that word; it means the same or almost the same thing. One definition is an *antonym*; it has the opposite or nearly opposite meaning. The other has a completely different meaning. Label the definitions S for *synonym*, A for *antonym*, and D for *different*.

_____ a. production
_____ b. destruction
_____ c. invention

2. Distinguishing Fact from Opinion

Two of the statements below present *facts*, which can be proved correct. The other statement is an *opinion*, which expresses someone's thoughts or beliefs. Label the statements F for *fact* and O for *opinion*.

_____ a. Natasha used layers of paint to create a wood-land scene.
_____ b. A painting created on a computer screen is not art.
_____ c. Andrew created and printed out his artwork in a few hours.

3. Keeping Events in Order

Two of the statements below describe events that happened at the same time. The other statement describes an event that happened before or after those events. Label them S for *same time*, B for *before*, and A for *after*.

_____ a. Natasha put the finishing touches on her painting.

_____ b. With a tap of his finger, Andrew sent the image to his printer.

_____ c. Andrew sat in front of a computer screen.

4. Making Correct Inferences

Two of the statements below are correct *inferences*, or reasonable guesses. They are based on information in the passage. The other statement is an incorrect, or faulty, inference. Label the statements C for *correct* inference and F for *faulty* inference.

_____ a. Andrew uses a computer to create art because he is too lazy to paint.

_____ b. Both Natasha and Andrew are creative individuals.

_____ c. Andrew and Natasha's mother does not want to show favoritism to either of her children.

5. Understanding Main Ideas

One of the statements below expresses the main idea of the passage. One statement is too general, or too broad. The other explains only part of the passage; it is too narrow. Label the statements M for *main idea*, B for *too broad*, and N for *too narrow*.

_____ a. Computers can be used to create works of art.

_____ b. Andrew and Natasha used different techniques and tools to create paintings.

_____ c. A work that expresses an artist's emotions and ideas is art, regardless of the tools used to create it.

Correct Answers, Part A _____

Correct Answers, Part B _____

Total Correct Answers _____

Coin Collecting

Almost since the first known coins were minted, they have been collected. The art of collecting and studying coins, other currency, and medals is known as numismatics. Some collectors are professionals. They appraise, purchase, and sell coins. But most people collect only as a hobby.

A good coin collection is an investment and can be profitable in a number of ways. As a pastime it provides hours of pleasure and the satisfaction of watching the collection grow. Moreover, coins—old, new, foreign, or domestic—will always be worth at least as much as the metals of which they are made. These are often precious metals. The retail value of a coin seldom drops below its face value. A United States cent, for example, will usually be worth at least $\frac{1}{100}$ of a United States dollar. The value of many coins can increase over time because the demand for these coins increases while their supply remains unchanged.

Coins may be of historical importance as well. The words and pictures stamped on ancient coins can be the sole source of information about the people who made them. Such coins may bear the only remaining images of famous historical figures or of buildings that have long since disappeared. An old coin is a survival of the past. It brings with it the atmosphere of the age in which it was minted.

The easiest and cheapest way to start collecting is to begin with coins that are still in circulation. Everyone carries a certain amount of change. Sorting and saving pennies, nickels, dimes, and quarters helps the beginner start a collection. From this start the collector learns which kinds of coins to acquire. Many beginners buy a coin folder for United States one-cent, five-cent, or ten-cent pieces and then fill it.

There are many other ways for a beginner to get help in starting a collection. Books about coins and coin collecting can generally be found in public libraries. Coin shops also carry books and catalogs containing valuable information about coins. A beginning collector can find other people who share a similar interest in coins by joining a coin club. Coin clubs are a chance for collectors to get together. They exchange information and trade coins. Some clubs hold auctions in which coins are sold to the highest bidder. More than 1,000 local groups have been started all over the United States and Canada.

Reading Time _____

Recalling Facts

1. The art of collecting coins is known as
   - ❑ a. numismatics.
   - ❑ b. mathematics.
   - ❑ c. metallurgy.

2. The retail value of a coin is usually
   - ❑ a. more than its face value.
   - ❑ b. its face value.
   - ❑ c. the cost of its metal.

3. The easiest way to begin a coin collection is with
   - ❑ a. rare, old coins.
   - ❑ b. 50-cent pieces.
   - ❑ c. coins in circulation.

4. A penny is worth at least
   - ❑ a. $\frac{1}{10}$ of a United States dollar.
   - ❑ b. two cents.
   - ❑ c. $\frac{1}{100}$ of a United States dollar.

5. Coin collecting can be profitable because all coins
   - ❑ a. increase in value.
   - ❑ b. are always worth at least as much as the metals of which they are made.
   - ❑ c. bear images of famous people.

Understanding Ideas

6. If the demand for a coin decreases while the supply increases, the coin will most likely
   - ❑ a. drop in value.
   - ❑ b. increase in value.
   - ❑ c. retain its value.

7. Coin collectors are most likely
   - ❑ a. impatient.
   - ❑ b. curious.
   - ❑ c. mechanical.

8. Numismatics is a hobby that requires
   - ❑ a. training.
   - ❑ b. wealth.
   - ❑ c. an interest in coins.

9. From the article you can conclude that coin collecting is
   - ❑ a. a popular hobby.
   - ❑ b. an unusual hobby.
   - ❑ c. limited to professionals.

10. A benefit of coin collecting is that it
    - ❑ a. can be profitable.
    - ❑ b. helps preserve rare coins.
    - ❑ c. forces saving.

In the summer of 1795, a teenaged Nova Scotia farm boy named Daniel McGinnis decided to do a little exploring. All his life he had heard stories about buried pirate treasure on Oak Island. He rowed out to the island to see what he could find. In the middle of a clearing on the island, Daniel came across an ancient oak with a sawed-off limb. Directly underneath, the ground had sunk to form a saucer-shaped depression. Daniel could draw only one conclusion—pirate treasure was buried here.

The next day, Daniel rowed back to the island with two friends. Dreaming of gold coins, the three boys began digging. Two feet (0.6 meters) down they hit a layer of flagstones. At 10 feet (3 meters) they hit a layer of oak logs. Deeper and deeper they dug, finding two more layers of logs before they finally gave up, 30 feet (9 meters) down.

Since that long-ago time, more than a dozen teams of explorers have dug in that mysterious hole on Oak Island. In 1803 one team hit a wooden chest at 98 feet (29.4 meters). When they returned to unearth it the next day, the shaft was flooded. They had sprung a trap that released the seal on a tunnel to the ocean. Vast sums of money have been spent on what has come to be called the Money Pit. But the mystery of Oak Island remains a mystery.

1. Recognizing Words in Context

Find the word *depression* in the passage. One definition below is a *synonym* for that word; it means the same or almost the same thing. One definition is an *antonym*; it has the opposite or nearly opposite meaning. The other has a completely different meaning. Label the definitions S for *synonym*, A for *antonym*, and D for *different*.

_____ a. mound
_____ b. sadness
_____ c. hollow

2. Distinguishing Fact from Opinion

Two of the statements below present *facts*, which can be proved correct. The other statement is an *opinion*, which expresses someone's thoughts or beliefs. Label the statements F for *fact* and O for *opinion*.

_____ a. People are foolish to spend so much money for nothing.

_____ b. The boys found a layer of flagstones 2 feet (0.6 meters) down.

_____ c. More than a dozen teams have tried to find buried treasure on Oak Island.

3. Keeping Events in Order

Label the statements below 1, 2, and 3 to show the order in which the events happened.

_____ a. Daniel McGinnis and two friends began digging on Oak Island.

_____ b. One team of explorers hit a wooden chest at 98 feet (29 meters).

_____ c. The boys came across a layer of oak logs at 10 feet (3 meters).

4. Making Correct Inferences

Two of the statements below are correct *inferences*, or reasonable guesses. They are based on information in the passage. The other statement is an incorrect, or faulty, inference. Label the statements C for *correct* inference and F for *faulty* inference.

_____ a. Many people have been willing to risk money in the hope of finding buried treasure on Oak Island.

_____ b. No one will ever find any thing of value buried on Oak Island.

_____ c. The three boys did not have the patience or the time to continue digging.

5. Understanding Main Ideas

One of the statements below expresses the main idea of the passage. One statement is too general, or too broad. The other explains only part of the passage; it is too narrow. Label the statements M for *main idea*, B for *too broad*, and N for *too narrow*.

_____ a. In 1803 a team of explorers sprang a trap and flooded the shaft.

_____ b. Since three boys discovered a mysterious shaft on Oak Island in 1795, many people have tried to solve the mystery of what might be buried there.

_____ c. The lure of pirate treasure has drawn people to search the oceans and seacoasts of the world.

Correct Answers, Part A _____

Correct Answers, Part B _____

Total Correct Answers _____

Flax has been raised for thousands of years. Ancient Egyptian mummies were wrapped in linen, which is made from the fibers of the flax plant. Records show that humans have eaten flax products for centuries, often for medicinal purposes.

Cultivated flax is of two types: one is grown for fiber production, the other for seed. Fiber flax grows tall and has few branches. It needs a short, cool growing season with plenty of rainfall evenly distributed; otherwise, the plants become woody and the fiber is rough and dry. To harvest fiber flax, farmers pull the plants up by the roots because cutting injures the fibers. Flax-pulling machines are used in the United States. Elsewhere, low-cost hand labor is used, which makes the imported product cheaper. This is the chief reason for the limited production of fiber flax in the United States. After harvesting, the flax seed is separated from the straw in deseeding machines. Next, the flax is retted, or rotted, in a pool or tank of warm water. Retting takes from four to six days. The water helps bacteria on the plant penetrate the woody stems. The bacteria ferment and break down the pectins, which cement together the woody and fibrous portions of the plant. The retted flax is then dried in open fields.

Scutching is the next operation. This process extracts the fiber, loosened during retting, from the remainder of the plant. The flax fiber is then combed to grade it and prepare it for the spinner. This is usually done by hand, drawing the fibers over pins to straighten them and to remove short, tangled fibers.

The long-line fibers make the best linen cloth. Linen made from these kinds of fibers is strong, durable, and moisture absorbent. It has a high luster. It is also resistant to microorganisms and its smooth surface repels soil.

Seed flax is an important crop as well. Farmers harvest seed flax with a combination mower and thresher. They then ship the seed to a linseed market. It is used in paints and varnishes and in linoleum and oilcloth.

The straw from seed flax was once a waste material. Now it provides the paper for practically all the cigarettes that are made in the United States. Many other specialty papers also are produced from seed flax straw. It is used too in upholstery stuffing, in insulating and packing material, and to make fiber rugs.

Reading Time _____

Recalling Facts

1. Linen is made from
   - ❏ a. the linen plant.
   - ❏ b. animal hides.
   - ❏ c. the flax plant.

2. The process of rotting flax is called
   - ❏ a. scutching.
   - ❏ b. drying.
   - ❏ c. retting.

3. The United States does not grow much flax because
   - ❏ a. growing conditions are poor in the United States.
   - ❏ b. imported flax is cheaper.
   - ❏ c. harvesting it is too difficult.

4. Seed from flax is used in
   - ❏ a. cigarettes.
   - ❏ b. rugs.
   - ❏ c. paints.

5. Fiber flax plants are pulled up by the roots because
   - ❏ a. the roots are a useful by-product.
   - ❏ b. cutting injures the fibers.
   - ❏ c. pulling is easier than cutting.

Understanding Ideas

6. If a fiber flax plant becomes woody, the plant may have
   - ❏ a. received insufficient rain.
   - ❏ b. endured a short, cool growing season.
   - ❏ c. been pulled up too soon.

7. In processing linen, bacteria are
   - ❏ a. useless.
   - ❏ b. indispensable.
   - ❏ c. dangerous.

8. The characteristics of linen cloth make it desirable for making
   - ❏ a. tablecloths.
   - ❏ b. veils.
   - ❏ c. lace.

9. From the article you can conclude that the flax plant is raised primarily for its
   - ❏ a. beauty.
   - ❏ b. usefulness.
   - ❏ c. food value.

10. Ancient Egyptian mummies were wrapped in linen, which suggests that
    - ❏ a. linen was the only cloth known at the time.
    - ❏ b. Egyptians were the first to make cloth.
    - ❏ c. Egyptians recognized the durability of linen.

Egyptian Linen

The ancient Egyptians grew high-quality flax and wove fine linen that they used for many purposes. One important use was in preparing their royal dead for burial. A body was embalmed and tightly wrapped in many yards of linen before it was placed in a highly decorated coffin. Bodies thus prepared are called mummies.

To prepare a body for burial, the Egyptians removed the brain and internal organs, soaked the body in a salt solution, and dried it. They filled the body cavity with balls of linen, often saturated with resin. Resin-soaked linen was also molded to form body parts to help give the mummy an attractive shape. The whole process took about 70 days.

Then the body was wrapped. The wrapping began with the fingers and toes and proceeded up the arms and legs to the body. The thin strips of linen were often arranged in elaborate crisscross patterns. Sometimes as many as 30 or 40 yards (27 or 36 meters) of finely woven linen were used in wrapping a body.

Grave robbers often cut and tore the linen wrappings to get at the jewels they thought many of the royal mummies wore. But much of the fine linen from royal Egyptian burials survives today in museums around the world.

1. Recognizing Words in Context

Find the word *saturated* in the passage. One definition below is a *synonym* for that word; it means the same or almost the same thing. One definition is an *antonym*; it has the opposite or nearly opposite meaning. The other has a completely different meaning. Label the defintions S for *synonym*, A for *antonym*, and D for *different*.

_____ a. drained
_____ b. soaked
_____ c. constructed

2. Distinguishing Fact from Opinion

Two of the statements below present *facts*, which can be proved correct. The other statement is an *opinion*, which expresses someone's thoughts or beliefs. Label the statements F for *fact* and O for *opinion*.

_____ a. The ancient Egyptians grew flax.
_____ b. The Egyptians used linen in preparing their dead for burial.
_____ c. Resin-soaked linen gave the mummy an attractive shape.

3. Keeping Events in Order

Label the statements below 1, 2, and 3 to show the order in which the events happened.

_____ a. The brain and internal organs were removed from the body.

_____ b. The body was soaked in salt water.

_____ c. The body was wrapped in linen.

4. Making Correct Inferences

Two of the statements below are correct *inferences,* or reasonable guesses. They are based on information in the passage. The other statement is an incorrect, or faulty, inference. Label the statements C for *correct* inference and F for *faulty* inference.

_____ a. Egyptians had elaborate burial practices.

_____ b. Linen was an important part of the burial process.

_____ c. People today have little interest in Egyptian mummies.

5. Understanding Main Ideas

One of the statements below expresses the main idea of the passage. One statement is too general, or too broad. The other explains only part of the passage; it is too narrow. Label the statements M for *main idea,* B for *too broad,* and N for *too narrow.*

_____ a. Ancient Egyptians made mummies.

_____ b. Mummies were always wrapped in yards of linen before they were placed in their coffins.

_____ c. Ancient Egyptians used linen in many ways in the preparation of bodies for burial.

Correct Answers, Part A _____

Correct Answers, Part B _____

Total Correct Answers _____

Each planet, including Earth, travels around the Sun in a regular orbit. Ancient astronomers thought that the orbits of the planets were circular. It is now known that the orbits are elliptical, though the orbits of most planets are almost circular. The extent to which Earth departs from a perfectly circular path is very slight. The orbits of Mercury and Mars are more eccentric, but Pluto is the only planet that has a markedly elliptical orbit.

The planets nearest to the sun move faster than do those farther away. Mercury, the closest, orbits the sun in about three months. Pluto, the most distant planet, takes 248 years to make one trip around the sun.

To people on Earth, the planet seems steady and immovable. Because it gives no sensation of motion, it is hard to realize how rapidly it moves through space in its orbit around the sun. Earth takes a whole year to make one round trip, which seems rather slow. On the average, however, it moves at 18.5 miles (29.8 kilometers) per second, or 66,600 miles (107,226 kilometers) per hour.

While Earth and the other planets move around the Sun, the Sun itself moves through a galaxy, or large group of stars, called the Milky Way. The Milky Way is a collection of about a hundred billion stars. They are arranged in a disklike shape with a bulge at the center. This central bulge contains about three-quarters of all the stars in the galaxy.

No one has made exact measurements of the Milky Way. Scientists, however, can see other galaxies in the sky. By comparing what they see with what they know about the Milky Way, they can make rough guesses about its size and shape and the number of stars it contains.

The entire Milky Way galaxy seems to be slowly rotating. The stars near the center probably move around the hub faster than those near the edge, just as the planets nearest to the Sun move faster than do those farther away. The Sun is about two-thirds of the way out from the center of the galaxy. Astronomers estimate that the Sun with its planets takes about 200 million years to make one trip around the Milky Way.

The Milky Way galaxy is part of a cluster of galaxies known as the Local Group. This group consists of a total of 17 galaxies.

Reading Time _____

Recalling Facts

1. The orbits of the planets around the Sun can best be described as
   - ❏ a. circular.
   - ❏ b. elliptical.
   - ❏ c. eccentric.

2. How quickly a planet orbits the Sun depends on the
   - ❏ a. size of the planet.
   - ❏ b. planet's distance from the sun.
   - ❏ c. shape of its orbit.

3. The speed of Earth as it revolves around the sun is nearly
   - ❏ a. equal to the speed of light.
   - ❏ b. 7,000 miles (11,270 kilometers) per hour.
   - ❏ c. 70,000 miles (112,700 kilometers) per hour.

4. A galaxy is a
   - ❏ a. system of planets.
   - ❏ b. large group of stars.
   - ❏ c. cluster of orbits.

5. The Milky Way appears to be
   - ❏ a. moving further into space.
   - ❏ b. slowly rotating.
   - ❏ c. the largest galaxy.

Understanding Ideas

6. Presuming that all galaxies have the same number of stars, you can conclude from the article that the Local Group consists of
   - ❏ a. about the same number of stars in the Milky Way.
   - ❏ b. about 17 times the number of stars in the Milky Way.
   - ❏ c. half the number of stars in the Milky Way.

7. You can conclude from the article that the science of astronomy
   - ❏ a. is still in its infancy.
   - ❏ b. is vastly uniformed about the Milky Way.
   - ❏ c. has reached its limits.

8. The Sun's location in the Milky Way means that it is
   - ❏ a. clustered with most of the other stars in the galaxy.
   - ❏ b. located away from most of the stars in the galaxy.
   - ❏ c. moving into another galaxy.

9. In the time it takes the sun to make one trip around the Milky Way, Earth will have completed about
   - ❏ a. 100 million orbits around the Sun.
   - ❏ b. 200 million orbits around the Sun.
   - ❏ c. 300 million orbits around the Sun.

10. Since the Sun is about two-thirds of the way out from the center of the Milky Way, you can conclude that
    - ❏ a. it is the fastest moving star in the galaxy.
    - ❏ b. most other stars move faster.
    - ❏ c. most other stars move slower.

16   B   Voyager

One of the ways that we learn about our solar system is through space probes like Voyager. Voyager was actually two unmanned spacecraft, Voyager 1 and Voyager 2, sent by the National Aeronautics and Space Administration (NASA) on a twelve-year trip to explore the planets around the sun.

Scientists worked for years to set up the Voyager probe. Only once every 179 years do the planets line up in such a way that space engineers could manipulate gravity to whip Voyager from one planet to another. In 1977 planet alignment was just right. In August, Voyager 2 blasted off from Cape Canaveral, Florida. It was followed by Voyager 1 in September.

Voyager reached Jupiter in 1979 and sent back fabulous pictures of that planet. Its instruments sent back new details about Jupiter's moons and measured such things as planet temperatures and the clouds and swirling winds that covered Jupiter's surface.

In 1982 Voyager left Saturn and headed for Uranus, which it reached and photographed in 1986. In 1989 it reached Neptune, its final exploration site. In 1990, just before it headed for the distant stars, Voyager turned its camera back toward Earth and snapped a picture from six million kilometers out in space. In its viewfinder were Jupiter, Earth, Venus, the Sun, Mars, Saturn, Uranus, and Neptune.

1. **Recognizing Words in Context**

   Find the word *alignment* in the passage. One definition below is a *synonym* for that word; it means the same or almost the same thing. One definition is an *antonym*; it has the opposite or nearly opposite meaning. The other has a completely different meaning. Label the definitions S for *synonym*, A for *antonym*, and D for *different*.

   _____ a. disorder
   _____ b. arrangement
   _____ c. visibility

2. **Distinguishing Fact from Opinion**

   Two of the statements below present *facts*, which can be proved correct. The other statement is an *opinion*, which expresses someone's thoughts or beliefs. Label the statements F for *fact* and O for *opinion*.

   _____ a. Scientists worked for years to set up the Voyager probe.
   _____ b. The planets line up in the right way only once every 179 years.
   _____ c. Voyager sent back fabulous pictures.

3. Keeping Events in Order

Label the statements below 1, 2, and 3 to show the order in which the events happened.

_____ a. Voyager left Cape Canaveral.

_____ b. Voyager reached Jupiter.

_____ c. Voyager took a picture of the sun and seven planets.

4. Making Correct Inferences

Two of the statements below are correct *inferences*, or reasonable guesses. They are based on information in the passage. The other statement is an incorrect, or faulty, inference. Label the statements C for *correct* inference and F for *faulty* inference.

_____ a. A space probe requires many years of planning.

_____ b. Voyager sent back much new information.

_____ c. Scientists did not learn very much from Voyager.

5. Understanding Main Ideas

One of the statements below expresses the main idea of the passage. One statement is too general, or too broad. The other explains only part of the passage; it is too narrow. Label the statements M for *main idea,* B for *too broad,* and N for *too narrow.*

_____ a. Space probes help us learn about space.

_____ b. Voyager sent back pictures and measured such things as temperatures, winds, and clouds.

_____ c. The Voyager space probe gave scientists a closer look at many of the planets around our sun.

Correct Answers, Part A _____

Correct Answers, Part B _____

Total Correct Answers _____

Plants may be classified in a number of ways. A common classification scheme organizes plants into groups according to the forms in which they grow. Plants are called trees if they have tall, woody stems, or trunks, and are generally 8 feet (2.4 meters) or more in height. Shrubs are low, woody plants, usually with many stems branching off close to the ground. Herbs have tender, juicy stems in which the woody tissue is much less developed than it is in shrubs and trees.

Flowering plants may be classified according to the length and pattern of their life cycles. Annuals complete their life cycle in a single year. The seeds sprout, or germinate, and the seedlings develop into flowering plants. New seeds are produced and the parent plant dies. All this occurs in a single growing season. Annual plants often grow in habitats that are inhospitable during some part of the year. They survive through these inhospitable periods in the form of seeds, which can withstand environmental extremes. Many familiar garden flowers are annuals.

Biennials require two years to complete their life cycle. In the first year they produce stems and leaves. In the second year they produce blossoms and seeds and then die. During the first year they produce through photosynthesis the food reserves that they need to generate their flowers and seeds the following year. This group also includes many garden flowers, such as Canterbury bells, foxgloves, hollyhocks, and English daisies.

Perennials live for more than two years. The oldest living thing on Earth is thought to be a bristlecone pine that is about 4,900 years old. Wild flowers are perennial plants. All the common garden perennials, including peonies, irises, and phlox, were developed from wild species. Some perennials produce flowers and seeds throughout their lives. Others, however, produce flowers only once and then die. The American aloe, or century plant, for example, lives for decades while its stem and leaves grow. After 30 to 60 years the plant produces an enormous flowering stalk up to 40 feet (12 meters) tall. Soon after the flowers mature and seeds are produced, the plant dies.

Most perennials are annual above ground—that is, their stems, leaves, and blossoms die in the fall. These plants, however, survive through the winter by means of their underground roots and stems. Trees, shrubs, and herbs also live and grow in much the same way.

Reading Time _____

Recalling Facts

1. One way to organize plants is by
   - ❏ a. how quickly they grow.
   - ❏ b. when they flower.
   - ❏ c. the forms in which they grow.

2. Flowering plants called annuals
   - ❏ a. die after a year.
   - ❏ b. bloom once a year for 10 years.
   - ❏ c. thrive in difficult climates.

3. Biennials complete their life cycles in
   - ❏ a. half a year.
   - ❏ b. two years.
   - ❏ c. two weeks.

4. The oldest living thing on Earth is about
   - ❏ a. 500 years old.
   - ❏ b. 5,000 years old.
   - ❏ c. 25,000 years old.

5. Perennial plants live
   - ❏ a. for more than two years.
   - ❏ b. about five years.
   - ❏ c. forever.

Understanding Ideas

6. From the article you can conclude that many plants survive by
   - ❏ a. adapting to their environments.
   - ❏ b. migrating.
   - ❏ c. producing flowers.

7. The stage at which a plant most likely endures a harsh environment is the
   - ❏ a. seed.
   - ❏ b. seedling.
   - ❏ c. mature plant.

8. From the article you can conclude that the various classification schemes for plants are
   - ❏ a. continually changing.
   - ❏ b. based on different characteristics.
   - ❏ c. not scientifically organized.

9. A gardener who wants a different garden every year should plant mostly
   - ❏ a. annuals.
   - ❏ b. biennials.
   - ❏ c. perennials.

10. The best time to plant a seedling outdoors is
    - ❏ a. during warm weather.
    - ❏ b. when the flowers mature.
    - ❏ c. after they become shrubs.

Plants that Eat Insects

When settlers first came to North Carolina, they were fascinated by little plants growing in the Carolina swamps—plants that "ate" bugs. A British botanist named the plant Venus's-flytrap.

Flytrap plants are only about 5 inches (12.7 centimeters) high. They grow in poor soil that does not provide all the food they need. The plants augment their food supply with insects.

The flytrap leaf resembles a bear trap. It has a special hinge down the middle, a fringed edge, and tiny "trigger hairs." When an insect touches a trigger hair, the leaf halves snap shut and the fringed edges of the leaf lock together like bars on a cage. The insect cannot escape.

Typically, the insect struggles for an hour or so. Then juice flows from the leaf's pores. The juice digests the insect; the leaf absorbs the juice. In a few days, the leaf reopens.

Venus's-flytraps remain fascinating today. Over two million are sold in the United States and overseas each year. Many of the plants are illegally collected from the wild. Scientists fear that the flytrap will soon disappear from the wild and grow only in those areas protected by law.

1. Recognizing Words in Context

Find the word *augment* in the passage. One definition below is a *synonym* for that word; it means the same or almost the same thing. One definition is an *antonym*; it has the opposite or nearly opposite meaning. The other has a completely different meaning. Label the definitions S for *synonym*, A for *antonym*, and D for *different*.

_____ a. decrease
_____ b. supplement
_____ c. surround

2. Distinguishing Fact from Opinion

Two of the statements below present *facts*, which can be proved correct. The other statement is an *opinion*, which expresses someone's thoughts or beliefs. Label the statements F for *fact* and O for *opinion*.

_____ a. Venus's-flytraps grow in the Carolina swamps.
_____ b. The flytrap leaf has a hinge down the middle.
_____ c. People are fascinated by flytraps.

3. Keeping Events in Order

Label the statements below 1, 2, and 3 to show the order in which the events happened.

_____ a. Digestive juices come from the leaf's pores.

_____ b. The plant absorbs the insect.

_____ c. The leaf snaps shut, trapping the insect.

4. Making Correct Inferences

Two of the statements below are correct *inferences,* or reasonable guesses. They are based on information in the passage. The other statement is an incorrect, or faulty, inference. Label the statements C for *correct* inference and F for *faulty* inference.

_____ a. People have always been fascinated by curious plants.

_____ b. Flytraps are important in reducing the number of insects.

_____ c. The popularity of Venus's-flytraps may put them in danger.

5. Understanding Main Ideas

One of the statements below expresses the main idea of the passage. One statement is too general, or too broad. The other explains only part of the passage; it is too narrow. Label the statements M for *main idea,* B for *too broad,* and N for *too narrow.*

_____ a. Plants can be very interesting.

_____ b. A Venus's-flytrap catches insects by trapping them with its leaves.

_____ c. Venus's-flytraps, native plants that trap and digest insects, have fascinated people since they were discovered.

Correct Answers, Part A _____

Correct Answers, Part B _____

Total Correct Answers _____

The sport of boxing is the art of attack and defense with the fists. Some people feel that boxing is too violent and dangerous and should be abolished. It has, however, endured in one form or another since ancient times and has a devoted following.

Boxing matches take place in a ring. The ring is a square platform (often called the squared circle), padded and covered with canvas. It ranges from 16 to 20 feet (4.9 to 6 meters) square in professional contests and from 12 to 20 feet (4 to 6 meters) square in amateur contests. Multiple lengths of rope attached to posts in each corner enclose the ring. Each fighter has his own corner, diagonally across from his opponent's. The other two corners are neutral.

If a fighter falls or is knocked down, he must get to his feet within 10 seconds. The referee counts seconds aloud as long as the fighter remains down. If the referee reaches the number 10, he declares a knockout (KO). Sometimes a fighter is hopelessly beaten without being counted out. The referee then awards the bout to his opponent on a technical knockout (TKO).

The bout is decided on points if neither contestant has suffered a knockout or a technical knockout or has been disqualified by a foul. Points are scored for the number of blows landed, for a clever defense, and for aggressiveness. The decision is reached by a majority vote of the judges on the basis of total points scored.

A good offense is built around four classes of punches—jab, straight blow, hook or cross, and uppercut. The jab is a sharp, light punch delivered by straightening out the bent arm. It can be used effectively to harass an opponent and keep him off-balance. A straight punch may carry the weight of the body behind it and will result in a knockout if landed in a vital spot. The hook or cross, either left or right, is a swinging blow, aimed to slip by the opponent's guard. The uppercut is a blow directed upward, usually aimed at the jaw or the midsection.

Clever moves are also useful to a boxer. Feinting is bluffing with one hand before delivering a blow with the other. Leading is opening an attack, usually with a left jab. Countering is throwing a hard punch at the opponent at the exact moment he leads off.

Reading Time _____

Recalling Facts

1. The ring where boxing matches take place is often called the
   - ❑ a. canvas.
   - ❑ b. squared circle.
   - ❑ c. corner.

2. A technical knockout is when a fighter
   - ❑ a. is knocked out.
   - ❑ b. is beaten without being counted out.
   - ❑ c. remains down after ten seconds.

3. If neither contestant is knocked out, the winner is picked
   - ❑ a. by the audience.
   - ❑ b. by the referee.
   - ❑ c. on the basis of total points scored.

4. The punch that is directed upward is called the
   - ❑ a. jab.
   - ❑ b. straight punch.
   - ❑ c. uppercut.

5. Bluffing with one hand before delivering a blow with the other is called
   - ❑ a. leading.
   - ❑ b. countering.
   - ❑ c. feinting.

Understanding Ideas

6. From the article you can conclude that boxing has endured because
   - ❑ a. supporters of the sport outnumber its opponents.
   - ❑ b. opponents of the sport outnumber its supporters.
   - ❑ c. the sport has received good publicity.

7. Judges are important in boxing because they
   - ❑ a. control the type of fighting.
   - ❑ b. make sure no one is hurt.
   - ❑ c. can choose the winner.

8. People who are against boxing are fearful that
   - ❑ a. boxers will get hurt.
   - ❑ b. people in the audience will get hurt.
   - ❑ c. the sport will lose money.

9. Boxing is different from other sports in that
   - ❑ a. the opponents are usually men.
   - ❑ b. one opponent tries to physically harm another.
   - ❑ c. the smartest person wins.

10. From the article you can conclude that the purpose of a technical knockout is to
    - ❑ a. shorten the length of a match.
    - ❑ b. prevent a losing boxer from being seriously hurt.
    - ❑ c. encourage good sportsmanship.

18   B   The Prizefighter and the Kangaroo

Throughout history, there have been many boxing matches and mismatches, but perhaps none so strange as the match that occurred in Atlantic City, New Jersey, on July 23, 1939, between "Two Ton" Tony Galento and Peter the Great, a kangaroo.

Galento had impeccable credentials as a heavyweight prizefighter, having even once knocked down the great champion Joe Louis. After his boxing career ended, Galento turned to wrestling. But boxing was his first love. "I'll fight anyone—and anything," he boasted. When a fight promoter offered him a match with Peter, Galento accepted.

At the bell, Galento came out swinging and gave Peter a hard left to the midsection. Peter responded with a right, dropped to the canvas, and kicked Galento hard. Warned against low blows, the kangaroo danced around the ring until the round ended as Galento tried to recover.

The kangaroo won the three-round decision. Galento asked for a rematch on the condition that the kangaroo wear boxing gloves on its feet, but the rematch never happened. Galento did accept challenges to box a bear and wrestle an octopus. Both matches ended in a draw. Meanwhile, Peter the Great retired from the ring undefeated.

1. Recognizing Words in Context

Find the word *impeccable* in the passage. One definition below is a *synonym* for that word; it means the same or almost the same thing. One definition is an *antonym*; it has the opposite or nearly opposite meaning. The other has a completely different meaning. Label the definitions S for *synonym*, A for *antonym*, and D for *different*.

_____ a. similar
_____ b. faulty
_____ c. flawless

2. Distinguishing Fact from Opinion

Two of the statements below present *facts*, which can be proved correct. The other statement is an *opinion*, which expresses someone's thoughts or beliefs. Label the statements F for *fact* and O for *opinion*.

_____ a. Galento once knocked down boxing champion Joe Louis.
_____ b. The fight between Galento and Peter the Great was a strange mismatch.
_____ c. The kangaroo won the three-round decision.

3. Keeping Events in Order

Label the statements below 1, 2, and 3 to show the order in which the events happened.

_____ a. The kangaroo kicked Galento.

_____ b. Galento agreed to fight a kangaroo.

_____ c. Galento asked for a rematch.

4. Making Correct Inferences

Two of the statements below are correct *inferences,* or reasonable guesses. They are based on information in the passage. The other statement is an incorrect, or faulty, inference. Label the statements C for *correct* inference and F for *faulty* inference.

_____ a. Galento would truly "fight . . . anything."

_____ b. The match between Galento and the kangaroo was not serious boxing.

_____ c. The kangaroo was the better boxer.

5. Understanding Main Ideas

One of the statements below expresses the main idea of the passage. One statement is too general, or too broad. The other explains only part of the passage; it is too narrow. Label the statements M for *main idea,* B for *too broad,* and N for *too narrow.*

_____ a. Tony Galento, who offered to fight "anyone—and anything," agreed to box a kangaroo.

_____ b. Prize fighting is dangerous.

_____ c. One of boxing's strangest moments was the match between Tony Galento and a kangaroo.

Correct Answers, Part A _____

Correct Answers, Part B _____

Total Correct Answers _____

Building a 10-Speed

United States manufacturers produce more kinds of 10-speed bicycles than any other type of bike. The price of a 10-speed ranges from about 100 dollars to 3,000 dollars. Price varies with the quality of the parts and the material used for the frame. The amount of handwork needed to construct the bike is another factor.

A cyclist may have a 10-speed bike custom built. The frame builder designs the bike to fit the person's height, arm length, and inside leg measurement. The designer also chooses the parts that make up the bike. The type of cycling for which it will be used must also be considered. A custom-built bike can be constructed to provide the maximum speed for every ounce of energy used by the rider. Most bikes, however, are made to conventional standards in sizes indicated by the wheel diameter.

A quality 10-speed bike is often constructed of lightweight high-carbon steel; however, some frames produced in the 1980s were made of plastic. The steel frame provides strength, rigidity, lightness, and responsiveness. The best frames are butted: that is, they are thick at the ends to give the bike stiffness and strength, and thinner in the middle for lightness.

The first step in frame construction for a 10-speed bike is to polish and connect the metal tubes of the frame. The builder cuts an exact curve into the ends of the tubes so that they fit together precisely. The tubes are joined by a device called a lug. Then they are fitted and held together by means of brazing. This operation requires extremely high temperatures. If not done expertly, brazing can weaken the metal.

The new frame is cleaned with blasts of compressed air. Excess joining material around the lugs is filed away by hand and the corners are smoothed. Next, each joint is inspected. Finally, the frame is examined for proper alignment.

A quality bicycle frame often receives five coats of paint: an undercoat, primer, base coat, top coat, and, finally, a lacquer. Then the front and rear forks are painted and fitted to the frame. Finally, the frame is clamped upside down and fitted with brakes, gears, handlebars, chainset, seat, pedals, and, lastly, wheels. The new bike is now ready for touring.

Touring is one of the fun activities in cycling. The best way to learn about touring is to join a bicycle club. Most clubs welcome new members.

Reading Time _____

Recalling Facts

1. The price of a 10-speed bicycle
   - ❑ a. is the same everywhere.
   - ❑ b. varies with the quality of the parts.
   - ❑ c. is determined by its size.

2. A custom-built 10-speed is built according to
   - ❑ a. wheel size.
   - ❑ b. who will use it and how it will be used.
   - ❑ c. conventional standards.

3. Quality 10-speed bikes are often made of
   - ❑ a. tin.
   - ❑ b. nickel plating.
   - ❑ c. high-carbon steel.

4. Brazing is a method of
   - ❑ a. weakening metal.
   - ❑ b. holding metal together.
   - ❑ c. cleaning frames.

5. The final coat of paint on a quality bicycle is
   - ❑ a. the top coat.
   - ❑ b. the primer.
   - ❑ c. lacquer.

Understanding Ideas

6. From the article you can conclude that custom-built bikes
   - ❑ a. cost less than conventional bikes.
   - ❑ b. are more expensive than conventional bikes.
   - ❑ c. cost the same as conventional bikes.

7. A bike racer would prefer a bicycle that
   - ❑ a. provides maximum speed for every ounce of energy the rider uses.
   - ❑ b. requires the most energy from the rider.
   - ❑ c. has the least weight and the largest wheels.

8. From the article you can conclude that the best racing bicycles are
   - ❑ a. painted red.
   - ❑ b. light in weight.
   - ❑ c. made of plastic.

9. From the article you can conclude that the most popular bicycles in the United States are
   - ❑ a. 2-speeds.
   - ❑ b. 5-speeds.
   - ❑ c. 10-speeds.

10. Most cyclists in the United States ride
    - ❑ a. custom-built bikes.
    - ❑ b. conventional bikes.
    - ❑ c. unicycles.

Building a Better Bike

Bicycle design changed rapidly until the 1880s and then just stopped. Since then there have been only small changes. Why has no one built a faster bike?

The biggest factor in limiting bicycle speed is wind resistance. Even hunched over the handlebars in racing position, a rider constantly hits a wall of air. In 1912 a French bicycle designer tried to solve the problem with a shell-like device that enclosed bike and rider so that wind would flow over them smoothly. In 1933 another French inventor offered a different solution—the so-called recumbent bicycle, which the rider pedals while lying down. Both designs were much faster than the standard bike.

In 1939, however, the International Cyclists Union banned shells and recumbent bicycles in all future events, discouraging design change. By that time, too, the automobile was diverting interest from the bicycle.

The International Cyclists Union, which oversees bicycle racing around the world, has not changed its ruling, but people keep trying. The International Human-Powered Vehicle Association, founded in 1976, encourages people to try new bicycle designs. They offer a $16,000 prize for the first single-rider vehicle that can reach a speed of 65 mph (104.7 km/h). Human-powered vehicle competitors feel they are getting closer.

1. Recognizing Words in Context

Find the word *diverting* in the passage. One definition below is a *synonym* for that word; it means the same or almost the same thing. One definition is an *antonym*; it has the opposite or nearly opposite meaning. The other has a completely different meaning. Label the definitions S for *synonym*, A for *antonym*, and D for *different*.

_____ a. attracting
_____ b. amusing
_____ c. turning

2. Distinguishing Fact from Opinion

Two of the statements below present *facts*, which can be proved correct. The other statement is an *opinion*, which expresses someone's thoughts or beliefs. Label the statements F for *fact* and O for *opinion*.

_____ a. Changes to the bicycle since 1880 have been small.
_____ b. In 1912 a designer created a bike shell to slow wind resistance.
_____ c. The recumbent bicycle was introduced in 1933.

3. Keeping Events in Order

Label the statements below 1, 2, and 3 to show the order in which the events happened.

_____ a. A designer invented a bike to be pedaled while lying down.

_____ b. The International Cyclists Union banned special bicycle designs in all events.

_____ c. The International Human Powered Vehicle Association was founded.

4. Making Correct Inferences

Two of the statements below are correct *inferences,* or reasonable guesses. They are based on information in the passage. The other statement is an incorrect, or faulty, inference. Label the statements C for *correct* inference and F for *faulty* inference.

_____ a. The International Cyclists Union has had a great influence on bicycle design.

_____ b. Bicycles will never go much faster than they do now.

_____ c. Someone may soon build a much faster bicycle.

5. Understanding Main Ideas

One of the statements below expresses the main idea of the passage. One statement is too general, or too broad. The other explains only part of the passage; it is too narrow. Label the statements M for *main idea,* B for *too broad,* and N for *too narrow.*

_____ a. The International Cyclists Union banned bike shells and recumbent bicycles in all events, discouraging design change.

_____ b. Although the International Cyclists Union does not encourage changes in bicycle design, people are still trying to build a better bicycle.

_____ c. Bicycles have not changed much in the last hundred years.

Correct Answers, Part A _____

Correct Answers, Part B _____

Total Correct Answers _____

The Amoeba

The smallest unit of living matter that can exist by itself is the cell. All cells consist of protoplasm, the "living jelly." The protoplasm of a typical cell forms three parts—the cell membrane, the cytoplasm, and the nucleus. The membrane encloses the other cell structures. The bulk of the cell's chemical work takes place in the cytoplasm, which surrounds the nucleus—the control center of the cell.

The most primitive form of animal life is a microscopic creature composed of just one cell—the amoeba. The amoeba has two kinds of cytoplasm: at the surface, a stiff, gell-like cytoplasm forms a layer that acts like a membrane. It holds the inner, more watery cytoplasm and its contents together. The outer membrane is flexible, taking on the shape of the more watery cytoplasm inside, which is continually moving and changing the body shape of the amoeba. The name *amoeba* comes from a Greek word that means "change."

The amoeba travels by changing its body shape. It extends a portion of its body to form a temporary foot called a pseudopod, meaning "false foot." Then it slowly pulls the rest of its body into the pseudopod. The pseudopod enlarges to form the whole body. New pseudopods form as old ones disappear. The amoeba also uses its pseudopods to surround food, which it draws into its body. The food remains in a bubblelike chamber within the amoeba while it is digested. Water flows into and wastes flow out of the amoeba through the outer membrane. The amoeba also breathes through its membrane.

If an amoeba is cut apart, it instantly forms a new membrane over the cut surface. Only the part containing the nucleus has a chance of surviving. The nucleus is also necessary for reproduction. To reproduce, the nucleus pinches into two and the amoeba splits evenly in half. The process, called fission, takes less than one hour.

Although an amoeba has no nerves, it reacts to its surroundings. It retreats from strong light, or from water that is too hot or too cold. If touched or shaken, it rolls into a ball.

Amoeba dwell in fresh and salt waters, in moist soils, and in moist parts of other animals. Common species are found in ponds and puddles and even in the human instestine. Most amoeba that live in other animals are harmless, but some are responsible for serious diseases.

Reading Time _____

Recalling Facts

1. The substance that makes up all living things is called
   - ❏ a. amoeba.
   - ❏ b. bacteria.
   - ❏ c. protoplasm.

2. The body of an amoeba is composed of one
   - ❏ a. membrane.
   - ❏ b. cell.
   - ❏ c. nucleus.

3. The activities of an amoeba are controlled by a
   - ❏ a. cytoplasm.
   - ❏ b. membrane.
   - ❏ c. nucleus.

4. An amoeba reproduces by
   - ❏ a. producing an egg.
   - ❏ b. dividing in half.
   - ❏ c. dividing into three parts.

5. The environment of an amoeba
   - ❏ a. has no effect on the amoeba.
   - ❏ b. causes the amoeba to react.
   - ❏ c. makes it reproduce.

Understanding Ideas

6. Pseudopods enable the amoeba to
   - ❏ a. travel and feed.
   - ❏ b. divide and reproduce.
   - ❏ c. take in and release water.

7. The protective membrane of an amoeba can be compared to
   - ❏ a. human skin.
   - ❏ b. a rubber ball.
   - ❏ c. a tree root.

8. Without its flexible membrane an amoeba would be likely to
   - ❏ a. fill itself with bubbles.
   - ❏ b. starve.
   - ❏ c. change shape.

9. The nucleus of an amoeba functions as a kind of
   - ❏ a. mouth.
   - ❏ b. brain.
   - ❏ c. arm.

10. From the article you can conclude that after an amoeba divides,
    - ❏ a. each half will eventually reproduce.
    - ❏ b. the nucleus dies.
    - ❏ c. one half will grow larger than the other.

Father of the Microscope

Born in Delft, Holland, in 1632, Anton van Leeuwenhoek was a merchant, not a trained scientist. He sold cloth. Microscopes had recently been invented. Leeuwenhoek thought he could use them to check the quality of the cloth he was selling. He began building his own microscopes. They were simple, one-lens machines—but quite powerful.

Once he had the microscope, Leeuwenhoek couldn't stop looking through it. Magnification made everything so fascinating! He put a drop of water under the microscope and viewed it through his lens. Creatures were swimming in it! Leeuwenhoek called them "cavorting beasties" and "living atoms."

Until Leeuwenhoek, no one had imagined the idea of microscopic life, animals so small they could not be seen by the naked eye. He immediately reported his findings to the Royal Society. The scientists gathered to reproduce his findings, and they, too, saw the tiny creatures.

Leeuwenhoek lived to be 85 years old. For the rest of his life, he continued to describe the things he saw—the structures of living things and, most of all, the tiny animals that we cannot see but which are all around us.

1. Recognizing Words in Context

Find the word *magnification* in the passage. One definition below is a *synonym* for that word; it means the same or almost the same thing. One definition is an *antonym*; it has the opposite or nearly opposite meaning. The other has a completely different meaning. Label the definitions S for *synonym*, A for *antonym*, and D for *different*.

_____ a. shrinkage
_____ b. enlargement
_____ c. movement

2. Distinguishing Fact from Opinion

Two of the statements below present *facts*, which can be proved correct. The other statement is an *opinion*, which expresses someone's thoughts or beliefs. Label the statements F for *fact* and O for *opinion*.

_____ a. Leeuwenhoek made his own microscopes.
_____ b. Leeuwenhoek saw creatures swimming in the water.
_____ c. The microscope made everything fascinating.

3. **Keeping Events in Order**

   Label the statements below 1, 2, and 3 to show the order in which the events happened.

   _____ a. Leeuwenhoek built a microscope.

   _____ b. Leeuwenhoek saw what he called "cavorting beasties."

   _____ c. Scientists saw Leeuwenhoek's tiny animals.

4. **Making Correct Inferences**

   Two of the statements below are correct *inferences,* or reasonable guesses. They are based on information in the passage. The other statement is an incorrect, or faulty, inference. Label the statements C for *correct* inference and F for *faulty* inference.

   _____ a. Leeuwenhoek's work moved science forward.

   _____ b. The microscope is a valuable scientific tool.

   _____ c. Leeuwenhoek was responsible for the success of the microscope in science.

5. **Understanding Main Ideas**

   One of the statements below expresses the main idea of the passage. One statement is too general, or too broad. The other explains only part of the passage; it is too narrow. Label the statements M for *main idea,* B for *too broad,* and N for *too narrow.*

   _____ a. The microscope made scientific discovery possible.

   _____ b. Under a microscope, Leeuwenhoek saw tiny creatures swimming in the water.

   _____ c. Anton van Leeuwenhoek used the microscope to make important scientific contributions.

Correct Answers, Part A _____

Correct Answers, Part B _____

Total Correct Answers _____

To the Rescue

With training, a swimmer can learn the proper way to rescue a drowning person. If the drowning swimmer is close to shore, a rescuer may throw a board, rope, or ring buoy and tow the victim to safety. If a boat is available, the rescuer may row out to the victim. A rescuer who is a strong swimmer with lifesaving practice may choose to enter the water to save the victim. Many people who drown do so because they panic and thrash about in the water. In their panic drowning victims frequently attempt to grab would-be rescuers to stay afloat. Rescuers who are not strong swimmers risk being pulled to the bottom with the victim.

One method of rescuing by swimming is to get behind the victim and pull her or him by the chin to a level position. With one arm, the rescuer then reaches over the shoulder of the victim and grasps her or him across the chest. The rescuer's free arm is used to swim a modified sidestroke. A shallow arm pull and inverted scissors kick are used to bring the victim to safety.

Like heart arrest and choking, drowning requires immediate action and basic life support. Near drowning is much more common than fatal drowning. The near-drowning victim may have no symptoms or may need help because of difficulty in breathing and confusion. The drowned victim will be unconscious and will not be breathing.

Water in the lungs results in a decreased ability of the air sacs to supply oxygen to the blood. The immediate problem of the victim is a lack of air rather than an excess of water. A rescuer should not try to pump or drain water from the lungs. Mouth-to-mouth resuscitation should be employed if the victim has trouble breathing or is unconscious, even while the victim is still in the water. If the victim's neck or back might have been injured, the rescuer should support the victim in the water in a level position until the victim can be eased onto a flat board.

Rescuers should not give up on a victim until she or he is pronounced dead by a physician. Getting the victim to a hospital quickly is vital. Humans have a reflex that slows the body's processes in cold water. This reflex can sustain life even though a person has been submerged for more than a half-hour.

Reading Time _____

Recalling Facts

1. If a drowning victim is close to shore, a rescuer should
   - ❑ a. enter the water.
   - ❑ b. throw a life-saving device.
   - ❑ c. pound the victim's back.

2. A drowned victim
   - ❑ a. usually calls for help.
   - ❑ b. is confused and gasping for breath.
   - ❑ c. is unconscious and not breathing.

3. Mouth-to-mouth resuscitation should be done when the victim
   - ❑ a. is not in the water.
   - ❑ b. has an injured neck.
   - ❑ c. has trouble breathing or is unconscious.

4. The immediate problem of a drown-ing victim is
   - ❑ a. an excess of water.
   - ❑ b. a lack of air.
   - ❑ c. a sore throat.

5. Humans have a reflex that in cold water
   - ❑ a. speeds the body's processes.
   - ❑ b. slows the body's processes.
   - ❑ c. keeps them afloat.

Understanding Ideas

6. The article wants you to understand that rescuing a drowning victim
   - ❑ a. is every swimmer's duty.
   - ❑ b. can be dangerous.
   - ❑ c. should be attempted only by lifeguards.

7. It is likely that rescuers are instructed to get behind a drowning victim so that the
   - ❑ a. victim cannot grab the rescuer.
   - ❑ b. rescuer can surprise the victim.
   - ❑ c. victim can stay afloat.

8. If a victim is unconscious, mouth-to-mouth resuscitation should be started right away because
   - ❑ a. the danger becomes greater the longer a victim is without air.
   - ❑ b. more water will enter the lungs.
   - ❑ c. the victim's neck may be broken.

9. If a victim has been submerged for much more than a half-hour, it is likely that the victim is
   - ❑ a. unconscious.
   - ❑ b. dead.
   - ❑ c. panicking.

10. Life support should be continued until a victim is pronounced dead because
    - ❑ a. it may be possible to revive the victim.
    - ❑ b. a rescuer can be sued by the victim's family.
    - ❑ c. dead victims can be brought back to life.

Saving a Life

Daniel Ortiz makes a common mistake. He jumps into the town pool, not realizing how deep the water is. When he can't touch bottom, he panics. He tries to breathe, inhales water, and starts to sink.

Lifeguard Bryant Kerns looks up and notices some splashing in the deep end. Maybe it's nothing, but Bryant's job is to make sure. To get a better look, he walks to the deep end of the pool and sees Daniel Ortiz sinking. Bryant yells for help and dives for Daniel. Another pool employee quickly dials 911.

Bryant reaches Daniel. Throwing an arm across Daniel's chest, Bryant pulls him to the side of the pool. Other hands help Bryant get Daniel out of the water. He's not breathing, so Bryant starts CPR. Almost immediately, Daniel starts coughing and throwing up water.

By the time the ambulance arrives, Daniel is sitting up. His lungs sound clear, but the medical technicians take him to the hospital just to be sure. As for Bryant, he repudiates any suggestion that he's a hero. "I didn't have time to think," he says. "I just did what I'm trained to do."

1. Recognizing Words in Context

Find the word *repudiates* in the passage. One definition below is a *synonym* for that word; it means the same or almost the same thing. One definition is an *antonym*; it has the opposite or nearly opposite meaning. The other has a completely different meaning. Label the definitions S for *synonym*, A for *antonym*, and D for *different*.

_____ a. concurs
_____ b. rejects
_____ c. understands

2. Distinguishing Fact from Opinion

Two of the statements below present *facts*, which can be proved correct. The other statement is an *opinion*, which expresses someone's thoughts or beliefs. Label the statements F for *fact* and O for *opinion*.

_____ a. Bryant walks to the deep end of the pool.
_____ b. Daniel is not breathing.
_____ c. Daniel makes a common mistake.

3. Keeping Events in Order

Label the statements below 1, 2, and 3 to show the order in which the events happened.

_____ a. Bryant starts CPR.
_____ b. Bryant notices splashing at the deep end of the pool.
_____ c. Daniel jumps into the pool.

4. Making Correct Inferences

Two of the statements below are correct *inferences*, or reasonable guesses. They are based on information in the passage. The other statement is an incorrect, or faulty, inference. Label the statements C for *correct* inference and F for *faulty* inference.

_____ a. It can be dangerous to jump into a pool without knowing how deep it is.
_____ b. It is not essential to have a lifeguard at a pool.
_____ c. Lifeguards are well-trained professionals.

5. Understanding Main Ideas

One of the statements below expresses the main idea of the passage. One statement is too general, or too broad. The other explains only part of the passage; it is too narrow. Label the statements M for *main idea,* B for *too broad,* and N for *too narrow.*

_____ a. Lifeguards save lives.
_____ b. Daniel Ortiz jumps into the deep end of the town pool and panics.
_____ c. Bryant Kerns's quick action and skill save Daniel Ortiz from drowning.

Correct Answers, Part A _____

Correct Answers, Part B _____

Total Correct Answers _____

Santa Claus, a popular character associated with the Christian holiday of Christmas, is said to live at the North Pole and to drive a sleigh drawn by reindeer. Reindeer are a subspecies of caribou, a species of deer. Caribou inhabit the far northern regions of North America, Europe, and Asia. In North America the woodland caribou is found in Canada and Alaska. The northern, or barren ground, caribou roam the arctic tundra. Greenland caribou—reindeer—inhabit Greenland and the far northern regions of Europe and Asia. At one time, caribou roamed northern Maine and Minnesota in the United States, as well as some Rocky Mountain regions. The last natural herd south of Canada disappeared in the 1920s.

Woodland caribou travel in small herds and migrate short distances. The barren ground and Greenland caribou move in very large herds, sometimes numbering in the tens of thousands. They move continually, migrating south for winter and north in summer.

Caribou have thicker bodies and shorter legs than most deer. They have brown coats and white tails, necks, and sides. The colors vary with the seasons, becoming lighter during winter. Those in the northernmost parts of their range may be almost white. Both male and female caribou have large, irregularly branching antlers. Females' antlers are smaller and more slender than the males' antlers. Male caribou also reach larger body sizes, some weighing more than 700 pounds (315 kilograms) with shoulders reaching heights of up to 4.5 feet (1.4 meters).

Caribou eat grasses and browse on low-lying vegetation. They are noted for consuming large quantities of a lichen called reindeer moss, which grows in the tundra regions. When alarmed, caribou break into a clumsy gallop, changing to a steady gallop that carries the herd across the tundra. They have large spreading hooves with sharp, cup-shaped edges. These give them a firm footing on the soft summer rangeland and on ice and snow as well. They are excellent swimmers and will often swim across a lake rather than go around.

Caribou are the most domesticated of the deer. Caribou hides are used to make clothing, blankets, and harnesses. In the arctic region of Lapland in northern Europe, the people follow the migrations of the reindeer, which have been largely domesticated. The reindeer provide milk, cheese, and meat. Unlike the fictional Santa Claus, the Lapps really do use the reindeer to pull their sleds across the snow.

Reading Time _____

Recalling Facts

1. Caribou
   - ❏ a. hibernate.
   - ❏ b. migrate.
   - ❏ c. nest.

2. Caribou differ from most other deer in that
   - ❏ a. their colors vary with the seasons.
   - ❏ b. they have thicker bodies and shorter legs.
   - ❏ c. they gallop.

3. Caribou are noted for
   - ❏ a. their antlers.
   - ❏ b. consuming large quantities of reindeer moss.
   - ❏ c. their intelligence.

4. Most caribou in North America are found
   - ❏ a. in the United States.
   - ❏ b. north of the United States.
   - ❏ c. in Michigan.

5. Caribou eat
   - ❏ a. whatever they can find.
   - ❏ b. grasses and low-lying vegetation.
   - ❏ c. insects and small animals.

Understanding Ideas

6. From the article you can conclude that caribou in the far north become almost white
   - ❏ a. so that they are less visible to their enemies in the snow.
   - ❏ b. as they grow older.
   - ❏ c. to distinguish them from other deer.

7. From the article you can conclude that woodland caribou and barren ground caribou are
   - ❏ a. distinct species of deer.
   - ❏ b. subspecies of caribou.
   - ❏ c. vastly different from reindeer.

8. In areas with little vegetation, caribou would most likely
   - ❏ a. become flesh-eating animals.
   - ❏ b. die from starvation.
   - ❏ c. change their diets.

9. The Lapps' use of reindeer to pull their sleds
   - ❏ a. is probably a myth..
   - ❏ b. may be the origin of the story of Santa's reindeer.
   - ❏ c. explains where reindeer come from.

10. From the article you can conclude that caribou migrate to
    - ❏ a. escape predators.
    - ❏ b. avoid boredom.
    - ❏ c. find food and warmer weather.

The Caribou People

The Gwich'in people, Native Americans who live along the Alaska–Canada border, live mainly by hunting caribou. Each year, a huge caribou herd migrates 400 miles from deep in the Canadian forests to the coast of Alaska. There the cows give birth to their calves. The cows and calves remain there all summer. The area has rich grass on which the calves grow strong. Because they are also fairly safe from the bears and wolves that prey on young caribou, the herds thrive.

The Gwich'in people have built their villages all along the path of caribou migration. The caribou provide them with almost all of their meat. The Gwich'in are deeply attached to the caribou herds. They call themselves the Caribou people.

The place where the caribou dwell is also very rich in oil, and an oil company wants to drill there. Even though the oil will bring much-needed income to other Native American peoples and increase the nation's oil supply in general, naturalists fear that drilling in this area will diminish the caribou herds. If drilling goes forward, what will happen to the Gwich'in who depend on the caribou for their lives? No one knows.

1. **Recognizing Words in Context**

   Find the word *diminish* in the passage. One definition below is a *synonym* for that word; it means the same or almost the same thing. One definition is an *antonym*; it has the opposite or nearly opposite meaning. The other has a completely different meaning. Label the definitions S for *synonym*, A for *antonym*, and D for *different*.

   _____ a. increase
   _____ b. decrease
   _____ c. replace

2. **Distinguishing Fact from Opinion**

   Two of the statements below present *facts*, which can be proved correct. The other statement is an *opinion*, which expresses someone's thoughts or beliefs. Label the statements F for *fact* and O for *opinion*.

   _____ a. The caribou migrate to the Alaskan coast each year.
   _____ b. The Gwich'in people have built their villages along the path of caribou migration.
   _____ c. Many caribou will not survive oil drilling.

3. Keeping Events in Order

Label the statements below 1, 2, and 3 to show the order in which the events happened.

_____ a. Cows have their calves.

_____ b. Cows and calves spend the summer eating grass.

_____ c. The caribou herd migrates to the Alaskan coast.

4. Making Correct Inferences

Two of the statements below are correct *inferences,* or reasonable guesses. They are based on information in the passage. The other statement is an incorrect, or faulty, inference. Label the statements C for *correct* inference and F for *faulty* inference.

_____ a. Reducing the numbers of caribou will harm the Gwich'in.

_____ b. There are no good reasons to drill for oil where the caribou dwell.

_____ c. The caribou herds are an essential element in Gwich'in life.

5. Understanding Main Ideas

One of the statements below expresses the main idea of the passage. One statement is too general, or too broad. The other explains only part of the passage; it is too narrow. Label the statements M for *main idea,* B for *too broad,* and N for *too narrow.*

_____ a. People may need animals to live.

_____ b. The Gwich'in people rely so much on the caribou herds that they call themselves the Caribou people.

_____ c. The Gwich'in people may be harmed if oil drilling drives away the caribou herds they rely on.

Correct Answers, Part A _____

Correct Answers, Part B _____

Total Correct Answers _____

The Start of Language

Language can be defined as a system of sounds, signs, and gestures that represent the same things to all members of a group. These utterances are used to represent things whether or not the things they represent are present.

Symbolic language is considered a human skill. The language of animals is considered direct and very simple in comparison. It is thought to consist of responses to what can be detected by the senses. When a dog barks at a stranger, it is responding to the presence of the stranger. It cannot express its attitude toward strangers without a stranger at hand. Dogs appear capable of expressing only a few basic ideas—hostility, affection, hunger, the desire to stay or go, and a few others. Like many other animals, dogs seem able to communicate only about the simplest matters and in concrete rather than abstract terms. If a dog wants to go outside, it may scratch a door or whine. It cannot, however, express reasons it may have for wanting to go out.

It is not known when humans first discovered the symbolic power of language. There are, however, theories about this discovery. Most involve imagining a simple coincidence of events: A primitive man digs for clams on a beach. As he digs, he makes sounds. At one point, he bites into an especially tasty clam. The next sound he makes he associates with the pleasant experience of taste. He points to the clam and makes the sound again, reinforcing the sound with a smile of pleasure. His companions understand. Thereafter, they have a sound to use for suggesting that it is time to go clam hunting or for telling someone they have found a good clam.

However language was discovered, it was probably something as simple as that. Humans gave names to the things around them, and to their feelings, beliefs, and actions. These were words. Humans then developed ways to join these words together into sentences. They became able to talk about the clams found on the seashore even when the clams and the seashore were not present. They became able to compose poems and to make speeches with such words. Most important, they became able to think with words. Human thinking would be very limited if they could only use remembered pictures to create and share ideas; abstract thinking and communication is made possible with language.

Reading Time _____

Recalling Facts

1. A system of of sounds, signs, and gestures with shared meanings is called
   - ❏ a. abstract thinking.
   - ❏ b. language.
   - ❏ c. communication.

2. The language of animals is thought to consist of
   - ❏ a. responses to what can be detected by the senses.
   - ❏ b. instinctive gestures common to all animals.
   - ❏ c. abstract utterances.

3. Language can be used to represent a thing
   - ❏ a. only if that thing is present.
   - ❏ b. only if that thing is invisible.
   - ❏ c. whether or not that thing is present.

4. Most theories about how and when humans first discovered the symbolic power of language involve imagining a
   - ❏ a. long process in which humans mimicked animal language.
   - ❏ b. supernatural event that changed human history.
   - ❏ c. simple coincidence of events.

5. Names given to things, feelings, beliefs, and actions are called
   - ❏ a. definitions.
   - ❏ b. words.
   - ❏ c. songs.

Understanding Ideas

6. You can conclude from the article that
   - ❏ a. advanced thinking came before language.
   - ❏ b. language advanced human thinking.
   - ❏ c. without language, humans could not think.

7. The article suggests that human thinking
   - ❏ a. depends on language.
   - ❏ b. is more abstract because of language.
   - ❏ c. is limited by language.

8. Without words, recording ideas would be
   - ❏ a. impossible.
   - ❏ b. limited to pictures.
   - ❏ c. limited to scholars.

9. Sentences are
   - ❏ a. recognizable names joined together.
   - ❏ b. united feelings.
   - ❏ c. ideas joined by letters.

10. You can conclude from the article that
    - ❏ a. language was probably discovered by the Romans.
    - ❏ b. language is limited to humans.
    - ❏ c. no one knows how language was discovered.

Can Animals Speak Our Language?

All animals communicate in one way or another, but do they use language to do it? For many years, scientists felt that language was what set humans apart from other animals. Then, experiments with chimpanzees, our closest nonhuman relative, taught us that animals could learn, at least in a limited way, to use language creatively.

Researchers worked with baby chimpanzees that had been born in captivity. They raised them much as they would human babies, with toys and television. Later, they moved them to a comfortable laboratory.

Trainers worked to teach the chimps the same kind of sign language used by hearing-impaired people. Soon the young chimps were picking up signs.

Some people argued that the chimps were just mimicking what they saw. But at least one chimpanzee learned to name things she had not seen before by stringing together words she already knew, showing that she really understood the purpose of words.

At the National Zoo, researchers are using flash cards to teach orangutans symbols for words. Will the orangutans ever learn enough language to carry on a conversation with a human? No one knows, but the possibilities are intriguing.

1. Recognizing Words in Context

Find the word *intriguing* in the passage. One definition below is a *synonym* for that word; it means the same or almost the same thing. One definition is an *antonym*; it has the opposite or nearly opposite meaning. The other has a completely different meaning. Label the definitions S for *synonym*, A for *antonym,* and D for *different.*

_____ a. uninteresting
_____ b. fascinating
_____ c. intelligent

2. Distinguishing Fact from Opinion

Two of the statements below present *facts*, which can be proved correct. The other statement is an *opinion*, which expresses someone's thoughts or beliefs. Label the statements F for *fact* and O for *opinion.*

_____ a. Trainers worked to teach young chimpanzees sign language.
_____ b. Today, researchers are working with orangutans.
_____ c. The chimpanzees were only mimicking what they saw.

3. Keeping Events in Order

Label the statements below 1, 2, and 3 to show the order in which the events happened.

_____ a. Young chimps picked up sign language from their trainers.

_____ b. One chimp strung words together to name things.

_____ c. Researchers raised baby chimps like human babies.

4. Making Correct Inferences

Two of the statements below are correct *inferences,* or reasonable guesses. They are based on information in the passage. The other statement is an incorrect, or faulty, inference. Label the statements C for *correct* inference and F for *faulty* inference.

_____ a. There are many unanswered questions about language.

_____ b. Chimps are smarter than orangutans.

_____ c. Researchers are still actively exploring the question of animal and human laguage.

5. Understanding Main Ideas

One of the statements below expresses the main idea of the passage. One statement is too general, or too broad. The other explains only part of the passage; it is too narrow. Label the statements M for *main idea,* B for *too broad,* and N for *too narrow.*

_____ a. The language of animals is a subject for research.

_____ b. Some chimpanzees have learned to create words using sign language.

_____ c. Researchers use chimpanzees and orangutans to study the nature of animal language.

Correct Answers, Part A _____

Correct Answers, Part B _____

Total Correct Answers _____

24　A　Paints

The most important material with which a painter works is the paint. Paints contain coloring matter called pigment. Most pigments are colors produced from plants, soil, or minerals. Today an increasing number of pigments are chemically produced.

Each kind of paint has unique qualities and can produce some effects but not others. The artist must work within the possibilities and limits of the materials.

In medieval times most artists worked with tempera. Tempera is made with earth or mineral pigments moistened with water and then mixed with an albumen. An albumen is a water-soluble protein substance, such as egg whites, that thickens when heated. Tempera color is flat and slightly glossy. Because it dries quickly, it cannot be used to model or vary surfaces. Tempera is usually painted on wood that has been covered with plaster and worked to a smooth, hard surface.

Fresco is a process of painting with water-soluble pigments on wet plaster. It is especially well suited to large wall surfaces. The design of the painting is first sketched on the wall. At the beginning of each day's work fresh plaster is applied. In the process of drying, the pigment combines with the plaster and becomes permanent. Colors, however, are somewhat limited.

Oil paints were first used in the early 1400s. Oil paint has since become the most commonly used of all mediums. The pigments are mixed with linseed oil, which allows them to spread thinly and easily. Oil paints can be made transparent or opaque so that the artist can control the depth of effect. Paintings in oil have extraordinary brilliance and depth.

Plastic compounds such as acrylic emulsions have been widely used since the mid-20th century. Some painters prefer them to oils because they dry faster and can be thinned with water. In addition, they are said to be more durable.

Watercolors, used in the East for many centuries, have been in use by Western artists for only a few hundred years. The most common type is transparent, allowing the paper on which it is applied to show through. Because watercolors are soluble in water, a great range of values is possible, from very light to very dark. Brilliant effects are possible, and watercolors have a fresh and spontaneous quality. Unlike oil paintings, which can be changed and worked on over a long period of time, watercolors are deadened when they are reworked.

Reading Time _____

Recalling Facts

1. Paint contains coloring matter called
   - ❑ a. pigment.
   - ❑ b. albumen.
   - ❑ c. plaster.

2. Most pigments are produced from
   - ❑ a. linseed oil
   - ❑ b. plants, soil, or minerals.
   - ❑ c. eggs whites and water.

3. Tempera is made with
   - ❑ a. plaster and chemical pigments.
   - ❑ b. transparent pigments.
   - ❑ c. earth or mineral pigments and an albumen.

4. Fresco is
   - ❑ a. a process of painting on wet plaster.
   - ❑ b. a quick-drying flat paint medium.
   - ❑ c. the most commonly used of all mediums.

5. Oil paints have been in use
   - ❑ a. since the early 1400s.
   - ❑ b. since medieval times.
   - ❑ c. for only a few hundred years.

Understanding Ideas

6. The basic difference between oil paints and the other paints mentioned in this article is that
   - ❑ a. oil paints are not water-soluble.
   - ❑ b. oil paints dry more quickly.
   - ❑ c. oil paints have been in use longer.

7. If you want to have great control over the depth of your painting, the best paint to use is
   - ❑ a. tempera.
   - ❑ b. oil.
   - ❑ c. watercolor

8. If you want your painting to withstand frequent handling, the best paint to use is
   - ❑ a. tempera.
   - ❑ b. acrylic.
   - ❑ c. oil.

9. If you want to achieve a flat effect in your painting, the best paint to use is
   - ❑ a. oil.
   - ❑ b. tempera.
   - ❑ c. transparent watercolor.

10. The article wants you to understand that, when choosing a paint medium,
    - ❑ a. color and drying time are the most important considerations.
    - ❑ b. different paints are suited to different approaches and effects.
    - ❑ c. the water-soluble paints are always the best choice.

24 B Renoir

Pierre Auguste Renoir was born in the town of Limoges, France, which is famous for its fine porcelain. Young Renoir showed an early talent for art, so his family sent him to learn how to paint designs on dishes and vases.

Renoir went to Paris, where he painted designs on window shades and fans. He also took art lessons, and in the studio he met other young artists. One was Claude Monet, who became a good friend, and later, one of the world's great artists.

Renoir and Monet experimented with creating the effect of a color by dabbing different colors next to each other. The style they developed was called impressionism. But Renoir wanted to do other things. He went to Italy, where he developed his interests in drawing and painting people. His most famous works are those of the people whose portraits he painted.

In his old age, Renoir developed excruciating arthritis. But he did not let swollen joints stop him. He had his assistants tie his brush to his hands so he could continue to paint. His final paintings are done in wide, bold brush strokes and brilliant colors.

1. Recognizing Words in Context

Find the word *excruciating* in the passage. One definition below is a *synonym* for that word; it means the same or almost the same thing. One definition is an *antonym*; it has the opposite or nearly opposite meaning. The other has a completely different meaning. Label the definitions S for *synonym*, A for *antonym*, and D for *different*.

_____ a. painless
_____ b. painful
_____ c. external

2. Distinguishing Fact from Opinion

Two of the statements below present *facts*, which can be proved correct. The other statement is an *opinion*, which expresses someone's thoughts or beliefs. Label the statements F for *fact* and O for *opinion*.

_____ a. Renoir painted designs on window shades.
_____ b. Renoir's assistants tied his brush to his hands.
_____ c. Monet was one of the world's great artists.

3. Keeping Events in Order

Label the statements below 1, 2, and 3 to show the order in which the events happened.

_____ a. Renoir learned china painting.

_____ b. Renoir and Monet became friends.

_____ c. Renoir developed his interest in painting people.

4. Making Correct Inferences

Two of the statements below are correct *inferences*, or reasonable guesses. They are based on information in the passage. The other statement is an incorrect, or faulty, inference. Label the statements C for *correct* inference and F for *faulty* inference.

_____ a. Painting was a great love of Renoir's life.

_____ b. Renoir was not as good an artist as Monet.

_____ c. Renoir's portraits were exceptionally good.

5. Understanding Main Ideas

One of the statements below expresses the main idea of the passage. One statement is too general, or too broad. The other explains only part of the passage; it is too narrow. Label the statements M for *main idea,* B for *too broad,* and N for *too narrow.*

_____ a. Renoir's whole life was spent painting.

_____ b. Renoir's most famous works are of people whose portraits he painted.

_____ c. From an early age, Renoir found ways of expressing himself through painting.

Correct Answers, Part A _____

Correct Answers, Part B _____

Total Correct Answers _____

Cloth is used for more garments than any other material. There are three basic types of finished cloth—woven, knitted, and nonwoven. Woven cloth is the most widely used, but it is easier to produce a patterned cloth by knitting. The fibers of nonwoven cloth are bonded to a backing or locked together. Nonwoven fabrics may be created by using heat, mechanical energy, or chemicals.

The companies that produce finished cloth make up the textile industry. Most textiles in the United States are made in the South. The majority of these are exported for clothing manufacture in many other nations. Many garments are also made in the United States from materials imported from other countries.

Japan and the Netherlands also have large textile industries and sizable foreign markets. Most of the textiles that France produces are sold within the country. France neither imports nor exports much cloth. Textile industries have been established in a number of developing nations. Among them are Nigeria and Sudan.

Just as fibers are woven into finished cloth before garments can be made from them, so other materials must also be processed before they can be made into clothing. Animal skins are treated by a chemical process called tanning to make soft and pliable leather. Furs may be let out, or cut into small pieces and re-sewn into a long, narrow strip. Latex must be converted into finished rubber.

Many steps are involved in producing an article of clothing. Some of these steps may be taken even before the processed material reaches the clothing factory. First a designer makes a sketch of the garment. From that sketch a sample is made to see if the style is practical. If the style is approved, a pattern is cut. Then the pattern must be remade in several different sizes.

The pieces of a pattern are placed on many layers of cloth for cutting. The worker who cuts out a pattern uses an electric knife that can slice through many thicknesses of cloth at once. After they have been cut, all the pieces of a garment are tied together according to size and passed on to a worker who sews them. Many different operators may work on a garment before it is completed.

Finished items of clothing are pressed, tagged, inspected, and packaged. Then they are shipped to the stores that will sell them. They may be transported by truck, train, ship, or airplane.

Reading Time _____

Recalling Facts

1. Most garments are made of
   - ❏ a. paper.
   - ❏ b. cloth.
   - ❏ c. chemicals.

2. Animal skins are made soft and pliable by a process called
   - ❏ a. stretching.
   - ❏ b. tanning.
   - ❏ c. soaking.

3. The first step in making a garment is
   - ❏ a. the designer's sketch.
   - ❏ b. a sample product.
   - ❏ c. cutting the pattern.

4. Before garments can be made from them, fibers must be
   - ❏ a. chemically treated.
   - ❏ b. let out.
   - ❏ c. woven into cloth.

5. Cloth is cut for clothing according to a
   - ❏ a. formula.
   - ❏ b. photograph.
   - ❏ c. pattern.

Understanding Ideas

6. A textile can be defined as
   - ❏ a. clothing.
   - ❏ b. a manufacturing company.
   - ❏ c. finished cloth.

7. From the article, you can conclude that clothing manufactured in the United States is made from materials
   - ❏ a. produced in the United States and in other countries.
   - ❏ b. exported from France.
   - ❏ c. sold within the country.

8. From the article you can conclude that because France neither exports nor imports much cloth,
   - ❏ a. clothing in France is made of leather, fur, and rubber.
   - ❏ b. France produces as much cloth as it needs.
   - ❏ c. French clothing designers and manufacturers dislike non-French cloth.

9. Patterns are cut from many thicknesses of cloth at once to
   - ❏ a. save time.
   - ❏ b. make cutting easier.
   - ❏ c. produce different sizes.

10. You can conclude from the article that the textile industry uses machines to make clothing because
    - ❏ a. the finished product is better.
    - ❏ b. machines are fast and cheap.
    - ❏ c. people are lazy.

Until the 19th century, all clothes were sewn by hand. Then in 1830 a Frenchman named Thimonnier created the first sewing machine. It used a single thread to form a chain stitch. The French government bought Thimonnier's machines and began using them to stitch soldiers' uniforms. But tailors who had lost work to these new machines rioted. They destroyed Thimonnier's machines and almost killed him.

In America, inventor Elias Howe heard someone say that whoever invented a sewing machine could make a fortune. He set out to try, and in 1846 he patented a sewing machine that could sew 250 stitches a minute. The machine forced a threaded needle through the cloth. On the underside, the needle picked up a second piece of thread to form a lock stitch.

At first, Howe's machine was a commercial failure. Unable to sell it at home, he took it to England but was disappointed there as well. On his return to the United States, he discovered that other sewing machine makers were prospering, using his design. Howe sued to defend his patent and won a royalty on every sewing machine sold, finally making his fortune. All sewing machines manufactured since that time are based on Howe's design.

1. **Recognizing Words in Context**

   Find the word *commercial* in the passage. One definition below is a *synonym* for that word; it means the same or almost the same thing. One definition is an *antonym*; it has the opposite or nearly opposite meaning. The other has a completely different meaning. Label the definitions S for *synonym*, A for *antonym*, and D for *different*.

   _____ a. personal
   _____ b. business
   _____ c. total

2. **Distinguishing Fact from Opinion**

   Two of the statements below present *facts*, which can be proved correct. The other statement is an *opinion*, which expresses someone's thoughts or beliefs. Label the statements F for *fact* and O for *opinion*.

   _____ a. Until the 19th century, all clothes were sewn by hand.
   _____ b. Elias Howe patented a sewing machine in 1846.
   _____ c. Howe's machine was a failure at first.

3. Keeping Events in Order

Label the statements below 1, 2, and 3 to show the order in which the events happened.

_____ a. Howe heard someone say that the inventor of a sewing machine could make a fortune.

_____ b. Howe sued other sewing machine makers and won.

_____ c. Howe patented a sewing machine with a lock stitch.

4. Making Correct Inferences

Two of the statements below are correct *inferences,* or reasonable guesses. They are based on information in the passage. The other statement is an incorrect, or faulty, inference. Label the statements C for *correct* inference and F for *faulty* inference.

_____ a. People do not always accept progress eagerly.

_____ b. Howe's sewing machine was inferior in some ways.

_____ c. Howe always believed in his invention.

5. Understanding Main Ideas

One of the statements below expresses the main idea of the passage. One statement is too general, or too broad. The other explains only part of the passage; it is too narrow. Label the statements M for *main idea,* B for *too broad,* and N for *too narrow.*

_____ a. Elias Howe invented the sewing machine.

_____ b. Unable to sell his machine in the United States, Howe took it to England.

_____ c. Elias Howe took on the challenge of inventing the sewing machine and eventually made his fortune.

Correct Answers, Part A _____

Correct Answers, Part B _____

Total Correct Answers _____

ANSWER KEY

READING RATE GRAPH

COMPREHENSION SCORE GRAPH

COMPREHENSION SKILLS PROFILE GRAPH

ANSWER KEY

1A	1. b	2. b	3. c	4. b	5. b	6. a	7. b	8. b	9. b	10. c

1A 1. b 2. b 3. c 4. b 5. b 6. a 7. b 8. b 9. b 10. c

1B 1. A, S, D 2. F, F, O 3. 1, 2, 3 4. C, C, F 5. B, N, M

2A 1. c 2. b 3. b 4. a 5. c 6. a 7. a 8. c 9. b 10. c

2B 1. S, D, A 2. F, O, F 3. S, A, S 4. C, C, F 5. M, N, B

3A 1. c 2. b 3. a 4. a 5. b 6. c 7. a 8. b 9. a 10. a

3B 1. A, S, D 2. F, F, O 3. 2, 3, 1 4. C, F, C 5. B, N, M

4A 1. c 2. b 3. b 4. b 5. b 6. b 7. a 8. c 9. b 10. a

4B 1. A, S, D 2. F, F, O 3. 2, 3, 1 4. C, F, C 5. B, N, M

5A 1. c 2. b 3. a 4. c 5. c 6. a 7. a 8. a 9. c 10. b

5B 1. D, A, S 2. O, F, F 3. S, S, A 4. C, F, C 5. N, B, M

6A 1. b 2. a 3. a 4. a 5. b 6. b 7. b 8. c 9. a 10. c

6B 1. A, S, D 2. F, F, O 3. 2, 3, 1 4. C, F, C 5. B, N, M

7A 1. a 2. c 3. a 4. c 5. a 6. a 7. c 8. b 9. b 10. a

7B 1. A, S, D 2. O, F, F 3. 3, 2, 1 4. F, C, C 5. B, M, N

8A 1. a 2. c 3. b 4. c 5. c 6. b 7. a 8. b 9. c 10. a

8B 1. S, A, D 2. F, F, O 3. 1, 3, 2 4. C, C, F 5. B, N, M

9A 1. b 2. b 3. a 4. a 5. c 6. a 7. b 8. b 9. b 10. c

9B 1. D, A, S 2. O, F, F 3. 3, 1, 2 4. C, F, C 5. N, M, B

10A 1. b 2. a 3. b 4. c 5. b 6. a 7. a 8. b 9. b 10. b

10B 1. D, A, S 2. F, F, O 3. 2, 3, 1 4. C, F, C 5. M, B, N

11A 1. c 2. b 3. c 4. c 5. a 6. a 7. a 8. b 9. a 10. c

11B 1. D, A, S 2. F, F, O 3. S, S, A 4. C, C, F 5. M, B, N

12A 1. b 2. b 3. c 4. b 5. a 6. a 7. b 8. a 9. a 10. b

12B 1. A, S, D 2. F, F, O 3. 3, 1, 2 4. F, C, C 5. B, M, N

13A 1. a 2. b 3. a 4. a 5. b 6. a 7. b. 8. a 9. c 10. a

13B 1. S, A, D 2. F, O, F 3. S, A, S 4. F, C, C 5. B, N, M

14A	1. a	2. b	3. c	4. c	5. b	6. a	7. b	8. c	9. a	10. a
14B	1. A, D, S	2. O, F, F		3. 1, 3, 2		4. C, F, C		5. N, M, B		
15A	1. c	2. c	3. b	4. c	5. b	6. a	7. b	8. a	9. b	10. c
15B	1. A, S, D	2. F, F, O		3. 1, 2, 3		4. C, C, F		5. B, N, M		
16A	1. b	2. b	3. c	4. b	5. b	6. b	7. a	8. b	9. b	10. b
16B	1. A, S, D	2. F, F, O		3. 1, 2, 3		4. C, C, F		5. B, N, M		
17A	1. c	2. a	3. b	4. b	5. a	6. a	7. a	8. b	9. a	10. a
17B	1. A, S, D	2. F, F, O		3. 2, 3, 1		4. C, F, C		5. B, N, M		
18A	1. b	2. b	3. c	4. c	5. c	6. a	7. c	8. a	9. b	10. b
18B	1. D, A, S	2. F, O, F		3. 2, 1, 3		4. C, C, F		5. N, B, M		
19A	1. b	2. b	3. c	4. b	5. c	6. b	7. a	8. b	9. c	10. b
19B	1. A, D, S	2. O, F, F		3. 1, 2, 3		4. C, F, C		5. N, M, B		
20A	1. c	2. b	3. c	4. b	5. b	6. a	7. a	8. b	9. b	10. a
20B	1. A, S, D	2. F, F, O		3. 1, 2, 3		4. C, C, F		5. B, N, M		
21A	1. b	2. c	3. c	4. b	5. b	6. b	7. a	8. a	9. b	10. a
21B	1. A, S, D	2. F, F, O		3. 3, 2, 1		4. C, F, C		5. B, N, M		
22A	1. b	2. b	3. b	4. b	5. b	6. a	7. b	8. b	9. b	10. c
22B	1. A, S, D	2. F, F, O		3. 2, 3, 1		4. C, F, C		5. B, N, M		
23A	1. b	2. a	3. c	4. c	5. b	6. b	7. b	8. b	9. a	10. c
23B	1. A, S, D	2. F, F, O		3. 2, 3, 1		4. C, F, C		5. B, N, M		
24A	1. a	2. b	3. c	4. a	5. a	6. a	7. b	8. b	9. b	10. b
24B	1. A, S, D	2. F, F, O		3. 1, 2, 3		4. C, F, C		5. B, N, M		
25A	1. b	2. b	3. a	4. c	5. c	6. c	7. a	8. b	9. a	10. b
25B	1. A, S, D	2. F, F, O		3. 1, 3, 2		4. C, F, C		5. B, N, M		

READING RATE

Put an X on the line above each lesson number to show your reading time and words-per-minute rate for that unit.

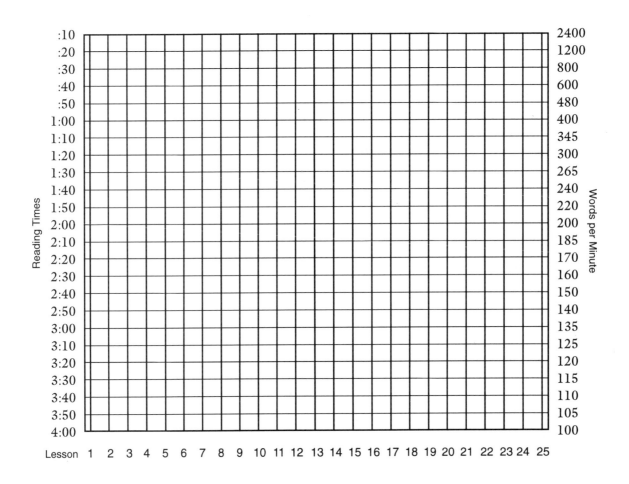

COMPREHENSION SCORE

Put an X on the line above each lesson number to indicate your total correct answers and comprehension score for that unit.

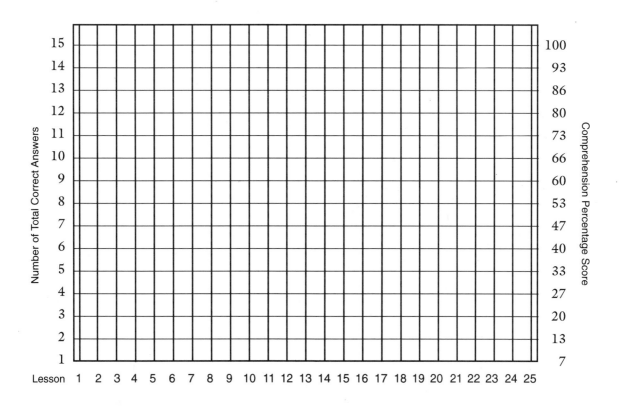

COMPREHENSION SKILLS PROFILE

Put an X in the box above each question type to indicate an incorrect reponse to any part of that question.

Lesson	Recognizing Words in Context	Distinguishing Fact from Opinion	Keeping Events in Order	Making Correct Inferences	Understanding Main Ideas
1					
2					
3					
4					
5					
6					
7					
8					
9					
10					
11					
12					
13					
14					
15					
16					
17					
18					
19					
20					
21					
22					
23					
24					
25					